NOTORIOUS San Juans

Blair Street, Silverton, at one time served as the red light district. *Drawing by Richard Turner.*

CAROL TURNER

NOTORIOUS San Juans

WICKED TALES FROM OURAY,
SAN JUAN & LA PLATA COUNTIES

Published by The History Press
Charleston, SC 29403
www.historypress.net

Copyright © 2011 by Carol Turner
All rights reserved

First published 2011

Manufactured in the United States
ISBN 978.1.60949.260.1

Library of Congress Cataloging-in-Publication Data

Turner, Carol.
Notorious San Juans : wicked tales from Ouray, San Juan, and La Plata counties / Carol Turner.
p. cm.
Includes bibliographical references.
ISBN 978-1-60949-260-1
1. San Juan County (Colo.)--History--Anecdotes. 2. Ouray County (Colo.)--History--Anecdotes. 3. La Plata County (Colo.)--History--Anecdotes. 4. San Juan County (Colo.)--Biography--Anecdotes. 5. Ouray County (Colo.)--Biography--Anecdotes. 6. La Plata County (Colo.)--Biography--Anecdotes. 7. Frontier and pioneer life--Colorado--San Juan County--Anecdotes. 8. Frontier and pioneer life--Colorado--Ouray County--Anecdotes. 9. Frontier and pioneer life--Colorado--La Plata County--Anecdotes. I. Title.
F782.S19T87 2011
978.8'25--dc22
2011013954

Notice: The information in this book is true and complete to the best of our knowledge. It is offered without guarantee on the part of the author or The History Press. The author and The History Press disclaim all liability in connection with the use of this book.

All rights reserved. No part of this book may be reproduced or transmitted in any form whatsoever without prior written permission from the publisher except in the case of brief quotations embodied in critical articles and reviews.

For Mardi

Contents

Acknowledgements 9
Introduction 11

1. Death of the Secret Service Man 13
2. Bad Blood on Bear Creek 34
3. The Grave Misfortune of Kid Adams, the Ouray Highwayman 40
4. Dangerous Women 47
5. Durango Desperadoes: Porter and Ike Stockton 58
6. The Tragic Tale of Mary Rose and the Cuddigans 71
7. The Famous and Infamous Days of the San Juans 77
8. A Colorado Range War: The Cox-Truby Feud 84
9. "The Utes Must Go" 94
10. The Wild and Wonderful Circle Route Stage 101
11. "White-Capping" in the San Juans 111
12. Tragedy at Pine River 117
13. The Sheriff and Marshal Shoot It Out 121
14. The High Price of Being (and Killing) a Gentleman 127

Notes 131
Bibliography 139
About the Author 143

Acknowledgements

Thank you to Sharon Stackhouse and Robynn Thomas, descendents of Joseph Walker, who shared their research, photographs and insights with me about the Walker case. Thanks also to their parents, Robert Tunstall Walker Jr. and Janet Robinson Walker, for sharing their family papers and photographs. I deeply admire the family's efforts to gain proper recognition for their ancestor's sacrifice. I also owe thanks to Julie Pickett, cofounder of Friends of the Animas City Cemetery, for sharing her considerable knowledge of the Stockton brothers and for sending me her shot of Isaac "Ike" Stockton's grave in that cemetery. A big thank-you goes to Ron Moore and the folks at Durango's Greenmount Cemetery for allowing me to use a number of photographs from their excellent website. Thanks also to Lindsay Eppich, for her photographs (and for digging through the snow); to Richard Turner, for his fine drawings; and to John and Lynn Turner and Jolie Gallagher, for feedback on the manuscript. Thanks to Elena Cline at the Colorado State Archives for her help with the mug shots and to the wonderful folks who run the Colorado Historic Newspapers Collection. Finally, many thanks go to Becky LeJeune, acquisitions editor at The History Press, who is a joy to work with.

Photos from the Walker family collection are courtesy of Robert Tunstall Walker Jr., Janet Robinson Walker, Sharon Stackhouse and Robynn Thomas.

Introduction

It took a certain kind of person to come to the remote regions of the west and build a life. As shown by the tragic story of a man like Thomas Greatorex, good breeding and civic mindedness were not always appreciated or rewarded. On the other hand, plenty of unruly fellows, like Ike Stockton or Kid Adams, found out the hard way that living beyond the boundaries of a regulated society was not always a free pass to raise hell. Justice in the San Juans was certainly uneven. Even if you murdered someone in cold blood, there was a good chance you'd spend only a few years in prison for your crime. That is, if you somehow managed to avoid being lynched.

The events in *Notorious San Juans* took place in three counties: Ouray, San Juan and La Plata. The source material was primarily the regional newspapers, of which there were many. Oftentimes, the newspaper publishers themselves served as more than just recorders—several of them played a major role in the drama. None of them shied away from controversy or taking sides. With at least one notable exception, they all seemed to have a jolly good time.

Chapter 1

Death of the Secret Service Man

On a quiet Sunday morning, November 3, 1907, four men explored a hilly area of homestead claims near Hesperus, eleven miles west of Durango. Two of the men were locals, hired as government contractors. The other two served as agents of the U.S. Secret Service. The men had come to investigate an unexplained air shaft—something that made no sense on a farmer's homestead claim.

They located the air shaft, placed a sturdy log across the opening and then rigged a rope and pulley. To test for air, they lowered a candle. Within five feet of the top, a draft extinguished the flame. Three of the men lowered themselves down the sixty-five-foot shaft. The fourth, Agent Joseph A. Walker, stayed up top.

When the men reached the bottom, they discovered a three-foot-wide opening to a horizontal tunnel. They entered and crawled for about twenty-five feet. As described by Agent Thomas J. Callaghan, "We were very much surprised to find ourselves in the main workings of a large coal mine."[1]

The area they had entered was the Hesperus Coal Mine, owned by one of the most prominent men in Durango, John Porter.

Joseph Walker, in charge of the investigation, had evidence that homestead claims in the area had been filed fraudulently at the behest of the Porter Fuel Company. In those days, homestead claims were inexpensive for settlers and free for former soldiers. The government placed limitations on where mining interests were allowed to buy land and charged them significant amounts for mineral rights. Reports had reached the Secret Service that some homesteaders were filing claims they had no intention of farming. Once they fulfilled the minimum legal requirements, they sold the property to a mining company.

The investigators spent an hour and a half inside the mine, making notes and measurements. It was a Sunday so the place was quiet. When they finished, they crawled back to the air shaft. There, they were startled to discover that the top of the shaft had been covered with brush. Much worse, the rope they had used to climb down now lay coiled in a heap at their feet.

They called up the shaft for Agent Walker but got no reply.

Realizing they could be in deep trouble, the men took the precaution of writing down the circumstances of their situation. They hid these documents among their clothing.

One of the contractors, Tom Harper, was the man who first alerted the agency to the air shaft. A former miner, forty-one-year-old Harper was a rancher and stockman living with his wife and three children in Ridges Basin. He had been hired by Walker only a few days earlier to help the investigation. Described by Agent Callaghan as a "big husky fellow," Harper announced that he was going to climb freehand up the sixty-five-foot shaft. The shaft was lined with round logs, so there was some footing available but little to grab onto with one's hands.

Harper began his climb and made it up ten or fifteen feet but came crashing back down again. He repeated this effort several times. Finally, amazingly, he somehow made it to the top. He lowered a tape line, to which the others attached the rope. When the rope was once again in place, the two other men climbed back up the shaft.

When they emerged into the sunlight, Harper gestured toward a nearby dump. Agent Callaghan was stunned to see Joseph Walker lying on his back on top of the dump. He was bloody and riddled with buckshot. His gun lay beside him, his hands rested at his sides. Blotches of blood decorated the immediate area; the largest, four to five inches across, was several feet away. Agent Joseph Walker was dead.

Aware that the shooter might still be lurking around, the men quickly split up. Tom Harper headed to a nearby farmhouse to call local law enforcement. The other contractor, John Chapson, was a civil engineer and geologist attached to the Department of the Interior. Forty-eight years old, he lived with his brother

Tom Harper *(right)* somehow climbed freehand up the sixty-five-foot airshaft. The man on the left could be Walker. *Courtesy Dan and Donna Harper, Durango, Colorado.*

Secret Service agent Thomas J. Callaghan made it out of the airshaft only to discover his colleague, Joseph Walker, lying dead in the dirt. *Courtesy Library of Congress.*

and father on a ranch on the San Juan River northeast of Pagosa Springs. While the others ran to get help, he stood guard over Agent Walker's body.

Meanwhile, Agent Callaghan rode their one horse toward Durango. On his way, he encountered two men in a buggy, and he noticed that one of them was carrying a shotgun. When he asked them what they were doing, the men were evasive enough that Callaghan grew suspicious. He ordered them to accompany him into Durango.

A little farther on, the party met two other men, both associated with the Hesperus Coal Mine. One of the men, Charles Johnson, was a celebrated lawyer in the region; Hesperus was his client. These two had apparently been looking for the two men in the buggy, and they joined the party as they continued on to Durango. As they traveled, Attorney Charles Johnson gave the men in the buggy an earful, but Agent Callaghan reportedly could not overhear their conversation.

It wasn't long before the group met yet another pair of men. This time it was local law enforcement: Sheriff Thomas Clarke and District Attorney James A. Pulliam. According to Agent Callaghan:

> *They stated they had received a call that a man had been murdered and that the fatal shooting was done by one Joseph Vanderweide, one of the occupants of the buggy, and that his accomplice was William R. Mason, Superintendent of the Porter Fuel Company, and whose homestead claim we were investigating that day.*[2]

Sheriff Clarke arrested the men in the buggy—William Mason and Joseph Vanderweide—and the group headed into Durango together.

A miner at Hesperus, Joseph Vanderweide admitted under questioning that he had shot Joseph Walker. He told Sheriff Clarke that he and Superintendent Mason had been out rabbit hunting together. He said they encountered Joseph Walker sitting on top of the dump. Walker allegedly threatened Mason with his revolver, so Vanderweide shot him with his double-barreled shotgun from about ten feet away. When Sheriff Clarke questioned him about why he would go rabbit hunting with buckshot, he answered that he expected to see coyotes.[3]

It took some work for authorities to untangle the events leading up to the death of Agent Walker, and his homicide caused reverberations not just throughout the San Juans and Colorado but all the way to Washington, D.C. Before everything was said and done, legislators in the distant capital would write new laws, and contemporaries would witness the birth of a new federal agency.

Fifty-one-year-old Joseph A. Walker had worked for the United States Secret Service for eighteen years, nearly half the agency's history. The Secret Service was founded in 1865 to fight counterfeit currency, and that had been Walker's specialty through much of his distinguished career. In the 1880s, he had moved with his wife and son to Denver. There he served as the first agent in charge (AIC) of the Denver Field Office, which covered Idaho, Montana, Utah, Wyoming and Colorado, along with the territories of New Mexico and Arizona. When the land fraud allegations began to surface, Walker was assigned to investigate. While his wife stayed in Denver, he spent much of his time in the Durango area. There his investigations had produced as many as 1,400 indictments. One of the indictments was against John Porter of the Porter Fuel Company. Although Porter had recently sold the mine to the Union Pacific Fuel Company, he was owner of the Hesperus Mine when the indictments were handed down.

Joseph Walker, shown here as a young man, started his career with the Secret Service in Washington, D.C. *Walker family collection.*

Walker came west in the early 1880s to run the Denver field office for the Secret Service. *Walker family collection.*

According the *Durango Democrat*, the investigations had not degenerated into open hostilities but had remained civil, due largely to Walker's even-tempered personality:

> *Of those who have been indicted, all speak of Mr. Walker as a gentleman in every sense. No officer could extend greater courtesy to those under investigation than he did. He bore the reputation of being exceedingly fair. But he possessed volumes of information that some people down in this neck of the woods wish had not been dug up.*[4]

When the story of Walker's death broke, newspapers across the state quickly filled with rumor, innuendo, accusations and denials. Conflicting stories appeared about many aspects of the shooting. The only details that everyone agreed on were that Vanderweide had shot Walker with a double-barreled shotgun and that Mason had dropped the rope and covered the shaft. Years later, Agent Callaghan wrote an affidavit, giving his theory about why Mason had dropped the rope:

> *It was afterward learned from a confidential source close to William R. Mason that their purpose in dropping the rope to the bottom of the shaft and making us virtual prisoners was to keep us there until they could return to Hesperus, procure some dynamite and return to dynamite the shaft, thereby obliterating all traces of Harper, Chapson and myself and claiming that whoever had descended the shaft had encountered a gas pocket, which through carelessness we exploded with our candles. The party, however, furnishing us this information refused to testify in court.*[5]

The morning after the shooting, Walker's body was brought into Durango to Goodman's Undertaking Parlors, where the coroner and several other physicians conducted a four-hour post mortem. The coroner reported six large buckshot injuries that originated behind the victim and to the left. The spread of the wounds was no more than eight inches, with injuries in the left shoulder blade up to the neck. Another shot had passed through the wrist of his left hand. One piece of buckshot severed his jugular vein, which caused his death.

Meanwhile, Durango and Hesperus became the focus of intense scrutiny, as government agents and journalists converged on the area. Excited reporters dubbed the case "one of the greatest sensations of the time."[6] On Tuesday, November 5, half a dozen high-ranking government officials arrived in Durango, and the head of the U.S. Secret Service, John Wilkie, was on his way. Wilkie and Walker were reportedly good friends. The Secret Service men set up headquarters at Durango's Strater Hotel and began conducting their own investigation.

On Friday, November 8, Vanderweide and Mason were arraigned. Both pleaded not guilty.

Many people in the area could not believe that Mason was involved. A respected pioneer family, the Masons had lived in the region since about 1880. Fifty-one-year-old William Mason had emigrated from Wales when he was twenty-eight. He and his wife, Emma, had a grown daughter, Annie.

John Wilkie, head of the Secret Service, considered the shooting to be a cold-blooded murder. *Courtesy Library of Congress.*

Mason's brother, Thomas, also worked for the Porter Fuel Company and later served for thirty years as treasurer for La Plata County.

Thirty-one-year-old Joseph Vanderweide had been in the area less time. From Atchison, Kansas, he had worked as a miner for the Hesperus mine for four years and his wife, Viola, ran a boardinghouse in Hesperus. The couple had a five-year-old son, Arthur.

Much discussion rose in the press over Mason's and Vanderweide's defense. Attorneys' fees were apparently being paid by the new owners of the Hesperus mine, the Union Pacific Fuel Company. Originally, they hired the firm of Ritter and Buchanan and "that greatest of all southwestern Colorado criminal lawyers, the invincible Charles A. Johnson."[7] However, that company's general counsel objected to the arrangement because Charles Johnson and his firm were already representing John Porter and others under indictment in the land fraud cases. The company did not want that connection to "implicate the company's officials in the tragedy."[8] The

Union Pacific Fuel Company hired another batch of local attorneys to represent the defendants: Russell & Reese and Wilson & McCloskey.

Despite protests from the district attorney's office, Mason and Vanderweide were granted bail in the sum of $20,000 each. Friends of the men were said to be calling around town to raise money for the bond. The *Telluride Journal* reported that both men were released November 13.

Meanwhile, several agents escorted Joseph A. Walker's body by train back to Denver. Walker's wife, Alida Tunstall Walker, had been visiting friends in Palisades when she was told of her husband's death. Said to be prostrate with grief, she arrived in Denver around the same time as her husband's body. The Walkers' grown son, Robert, also traveled from his home in Arizona.

Joseph and Alida Walker were well known in Denver, and there was a great outpouring of grief and support for Alida. Members of the Denver Press Club, including twenty-three-year-old pre-fame Damon Runyon, issued a moving personal tribute to Walker: "As a friend he stood 'four-square to all

Walker's wife, Alida Tunstall Walker. *Walker family collection.*

the winds that blow.' He was always to be found with the word of sympathy for the suffering, and he never refused to aid with his substance a friend who had fallen on life's highway."[9]

Walker's funeral was held on Sunday, November 10, at Boulevard Congregational Church in Denver. He was cremated according to his wishes, and his ashes were buried at Fairmount Cemetery. Unfortunately, the law at that time did not provide a widow's pension for fallen agents, and Alida Walker was unable to afford a marker for his grave. Later on, as a direct response to Walker's death, laws were changed to create a pension fund for such cases.

The newspapers, meanwhile, had been lining up on opposite sides of the issue. On November 9, 1907, the *Durango Democrat* called the shooting "Cold Blooded Murder" and implied what many were thinking—that the laborer Vanderweide had been hired as the trigger man: "In the face of things this is…a crime in which common thugs do the dirty work, and general 'interests' undertake to secure the thug's immunity."[10]

The *Durango Wage Earner* eventually published an editorial attacking the *Durango Democrat* for its numerous articles decrying the land fraud and Walker's killing:

> *The great and inglorious* Durango Democrat *for months has busted its gall bladder, fuming, yelling and gesticulating its abhorrence of the land, timber and coal thieves of this section of the state. Oh, what glorification it has ascribed to itself generally and the doughty colonel* [David Day] *in particular for the part it and he had taken in smelling out these damnable frauds.*[11]

The editor then went on to suggest that Durango's citizens should boycott the *Durango Democrat*: "Is it right that a community thus spit upon and reviled should by its patronage help keep these yellow journals alive? Why not spurn them from your homes and refuse to let your wives and children see them much less read them?"[12]

The *Breckenridge Bulletin*, a more remote and perhaps more objective source, described the battle lines being drawn: "Walker's companions insist that he was murdered in cold blood, while friends of Superintendent Mason declare he would not be a party to anything of that nature."[13]

Wicked Tales from Ouray, San Juan and La Plata Counties

In the same paper, Secret Service chief John E. Wilkie is paraphrased as saying that "he was convinced from such details as are at hand that the killing was nothing less than cold blooded murder."[14] Said Wilkie: "I discredit this story [that Walker shot first]. Walker was not a man who was looking for trouble, and there is no reason why he should have objected to the hunters passing the mine."[15]

Wilkie had taken over Walker's duties in charge of the land fraud case. He wanted to try Mason and Vanderweide in federal court, insisting that local sentiment was against them because of the 1,400 land fraud indictments, and that they would be unable to find an unbiased jury in the area.

About three weeks after the shooting, federal judge Robert E. Lewis ordered a special session of a federal grand jury to examine both Walker's homicide and the fraud indictments. Forty people were subpoenaed to testify, including dozens from the Durango area. The hearings began in Denver on

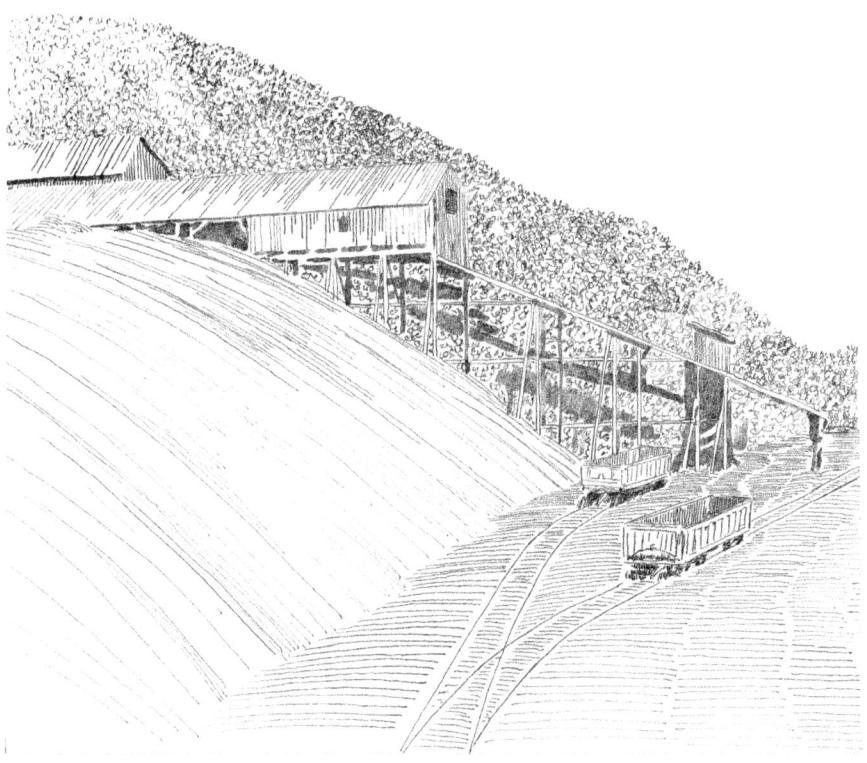

Hesperus mine buildings. *Drawing by Richard Turner.*

December 12 and lasted several weeks. In January 1908, to the amazement and consternation of federal officials and the delight of many in Durango, Judge Lewis quashed all but one of the indictments that had been handed down in the land fraud cases.[16] The *Durango Democrat* declared that "the killing of Jos. A. Walker is declared responsible for the tumbling down of the case which had been built up by the secret service men."[17]

The one remaining indictment was against John A. Porter, former owner of the Hesperus Coal Mine. The feds asked for a continuance for Porter's trial because they had not yet completed their case when Walker was shot. This indictment was also later dismissed.

At the same time, the grand jury handed down indictments against Mason and Vanderweide, charging them with conspiracy to assassinate Joseph A. Walker. However, Judge Lewis ordered that no *capias* (arrest warrant) would be issued until the men had been tried for murder by the state.

After a postponement or two, the murder trial of William Mason and Joseph Vanderweide finally began in a packed courtroom on April 20, 1908. Presiding over the trial was Judge Charles A. Pike. The prosecution consisted of District Attorney James A. Pulliam and his assistant, George W. Lane. Four attorneys composed the defense: James L. Russell, Willis A. Reese, Ben B. Russell (son of James L.) and Reese McCloskey. The two defendants were being tried together, and both had pleaded justifiable homicide. Members of the jury were: "Virgil Hammer, Bayfield; John Juby; W.J. Boyle, a miner; Al Bernard, Durango; Jacob Hargeshimer, rancher; Mart Busnell, Theatorium; E.V. Clark; N.B. Conley, Florida rancher; Marion Drury, blacksmith, Bayfield; A.E. Knapp, Globe Express; Thomas Farley, coal & express."[18]

The prosecution began with testimony that contradicted Mason's claim that he did not recognize Walker when he saw him by the air shaft. Walker's boss, thirty-two-year-old Lucien Wheeler with the Department of Justice in Washington, D.C., testified that Walker had introduced him to Mason during a meeting in Denver months before the shooting. Assistant Attorney General Frank Hall also testified that he was introduced to Mason by Walker. When Mason took the stand later, he said he didn't recognize Walker because the latter was dressed differently.[19]

Dr. John Haggert testified that he found a total of seven buckshot wounds in Walker's body, including two in the left side of his neck, two in his left wrist and three shots in Walker's back. The buckshot that entered Walker's back had passed through his lungs, causing extensive internal bleeding. Doctors removed two quarts of blood from his lung cavity during the autopsy.

Haggert's testimony took on new meaning when he stated that he believed there were two shots fired at Walker, which could have occurred since Vanderweide had a double-barreled shotgun.

Another doctor present at the autopsy, A.L. Davis, also testified that he thought the angle of Walker's wounds indicated that there were two or more shots fired.[20]

La Plata County coroner Herbert Lefurgey testified that some of the wounds were in the center of Walker's back near the spinal column. All the wounds had a downward trajectory, indicating the shooter stood at a higher elevation than Walker.

The trial heated up when Sheriff Clarke brought in a life-sized dummy of Agent Walker, dressed in Walker's blood-stained and buckshot-riddled clothing. Clarke gave a thorough presentation of the dummy, showing the location of each injury and demonstrating that Walker had been shot in the back.

All of this testimony tended to contradict what Mason and Vanderweide had told the sheriff—that Walker fired at them first.

The jury listened to extensive testimony about whether Walker's gun had been fired that day. A five-chamber revolver, it was found lying in the dirt next to Walker with four unspent cartridges in it. Frank Hall testified that Walker carried a Smith & Wesson .38 blue frame gun in an "Army scabbard."[21] Hall identified the gun, saying that Walker always kept it loaded with four cartridges, with one empty shell under the trigger for safety reasons.

The geologist who'd been with the group down in the shaft that day, John E. Chapson, testified that, as he stood guard over Walker's body and waited for officials to arrive, he examined Walker's gun. He ran a weed down the barrel to determine whether the hammer was on an empty shell. He found that it was. He also found 10-gauge Winchester shotgun shells about sixty feet away from the body. While he waited, several armed men from the Hesperus mine came down the gulch. He recognized them, but wanting to avoid trouble, he kept his distance, and there was no interaction among the men and him.

Another witness, David F. Camp, a marshal in Greeley, testified that he had worked with Walker on counterfeit cases and had known him for sixteen years. He corroborated Hall's testimony that Walker always carried his gun loaded with a blank shell.

Critical testimony for the prosecution came in the person of Lee Knapp, a Denver gunsmith. He had known Walker since 1893, when Knapp was on the Denver police force and Walker had often called on him to examine weapons. Knapp confirmed testimony from others that Walker never carried his gun with the hammer on a loaded chamber.

More importantly, Knapp testified that he had examined Walker's gun and determined that it had not been fired that day. He knew this because the empty cartridge under the revolver's hammer was not the cartridge that had last been fired from the gun. He said the cartridge under the hammer was a Peters semismokeless shell—the type that did not leave a powder residue in the barrel. However, the barrel was dirty with powdered residue, indicating that a black powder cartridge had last been fired through it.

> *He said, if a Peters cartridge had been fired through the barrel after a black powder one, the Peters one would clean the black powder soot out of the barrel.*
>
> *The district attorney here asked that Mr. Knapp be permitted to demonstrate this to the court and jury at some convenient time and place, but he was overruled.*[22]

Upon cross-examination by defense attorneys, the forty-eight-year-old Knapp admitted that he had never attended a school of powder or gunnery. He insisted that Peters shells were never loaded with black powder. He said that Chapson running the weed down the barrel of the pistol "might and might not have changed the appearance of the barrel."[23]

In what must have been a laborious process, the defense handed Knapp a series of nearly a dozen guns and asked him to identify what kind of shell had last been fired from each. Knapp examined each weapon and made a determination for the court about what type of shell was last fired. The defense later brought on a witness named Rowe N. Pingrey to testify about the results of these tests. He said Knapp had got the first gun wrong, and the second gun partially wrong, as it had been shot with both types. Pingrey's testimony stopped there. As explained by the *Durango Democrat*: "There had been 12 guns introduced by the defense to test Knapp's ability to testify as a witness on whether black or semi-smokeless powder had been used. The other ten guns were not introduced, which makes it quite evident that he must have hit it good."[24]

The next prosecution witness created a sensation in the courtroom. Santiago Gardunio had been convicted of manslaughter and had been in a jail cell near Mason and Vanderweide. He testified that he heard a whispered conversation between the two men at eleven o'clock at night, during which Vanderweide told Mason that "he [Vanderweide] ought not to have to stand it alone,"[25] and that he was worried about how bad it looked that Walker had been shot from behind. Gardunio quoted Mason as saying it wasn't so bad, that it "was from the side and wouldn't show so plain."[26] Mason also said that "Walker had to be killed, and if they did not do it, some one else would."[27] Mason talked about rolling Walker's body over and removing Walker's gun from its scabbard. Vanderweide asked Mason if he had fired a shot or two from Walker's gun, and Mason's response was that "there was one gone and that was enough."[28]

Under cross-examination by the defense, Gardunio insisted that he hadn't been promised that he would get out of prison sooner by telling the story. He said he had told Sheriff Clarke about the conversation before he was transferred to Cañon City, and the prosecution had brought him back from the penitentiary to testify. However, the defense got him to admit that he had told Mrs. Bates, the jailer's wife, that he had not heard anything. Gardunio said he had lied to Mrs. Bates.

Tom Harper, the miner who had climbed up the shaft, testified that in 1893, he had worked for the Hesperus mine for three and a half days and quit. He denied claims by defense attorneys that he had been fired for laziness or that he had taken a nap in someone's bunk while on the job.[29]

The prosecution wrapped up their case by bringing E.M. Snyder of Hesperus to the stand. The night before the shooting, Snyder had seen and talked to Mason. The DA wanted Snyder to testify about something Mason had said that night about "what he intended to do the next day."[30] However, the defense objected, saying that because Mason and Vanderweide were being tried together, any conversation that did not involve both parties was inadmissible. The judge sustained this objection.

Once the prosecution rested, the defense called Joseph Vanderweide to the stand. Vanderweide had been working as a miner at the Hesperus Coal

Mine for three years. He testified that he and Mason were "friendly" and stated "we have been together considerably lately."[31] He and his wife, Viola, lived about one hundred feet from Mason and his wife on the La Plata River in Hesperus. He testified that the night before the shooting, Mason asked him to go out with him the next day but did not tell him the purpose of the trip. When Mason arrived in the morning, Vanderweide decided to take his shotgun, though Mason told him there was no use for it. The two men rode around on horses for a time. Mason appeared to be looking for something, so Vanderweide questioned him about it. Mason said he'd heard that there was blasting in the area, and he wanted to investigate.

Vanderweide admitted that he had loaded his shotgun but said he did so because they had spotted a coyote. Finally, they rode up to a ridge, and Mason said, "I see a man at the shaft."[32] Mason dismounted and led his horse down the hill. Vanderweide followed, also on foot. Vanderweide did not know Walker, who "was sitting at [the] northeast corner of the shaft." Mason told Vanderweide to hold his horse while he went farther down. "When Mason struck the bottom of the gulch, Walker called to Mason to halt. He pulled his gun from his left side and again called to Mason to halt and fired. I then fired both shots at him, as quick as I could, to save the life of Mr. Mason, as Walker was about to fire again."[33]

Neither man examined the body. Vanderweide insisted that "I did not know whom I had killed and do not know now except from hearsay."[34]

Mason then went to the shaft and untied the rope. Vanderweide testified, "We saw clothes, pick and shovel at the shaft and concluded that others were down the shaft. We went to Hesperus and Mason telephoned to town what had happened."[35] There Mason sent some men back to the shaft to watch the body and ordered another man to guard the mine entrance in case someone came out.

Vanderweide denied he ever told Sheriff Clarke they were rabbit hunting. He also denied the jailhouse conversation reported by Gardunio. He said that Gardunio had asked him for advice, and Vanderweide pushed him away, telling him he wanted nothing to do with him. He said their attorneys had told them to expect spies in jail and not to discuss the case.

Vanderweide had never been in trouble with the law before and said he didn't even know about the land fraud investigations.

Broken chunks of metal and concrete mark the entrance to the Hesperus mine, today located on the property of Lane Folsom. *Photo by Sharon Stackhouse.*

When William Mason took the stand, he offered two reasons for the trip with Vanderweide. He said he'd been told that Tom Harper and others were blasting on company property. He had also heard that some Italians had been over on the Fort Lewis Mesa, hunting prairie chickens, and he was looking for them because he was a deputy game warden.

When DA Pulliam pressed him on which explanation he wanted to use, Mason got "mixed," as described by the *Durango Democrat*.

Mason corroborated Vanderweide's testimony that it was the latter's idea to bring his shotgun and that Vanderweide had loaded the gun when they spotted the coyote. Like Vanderweide, he denied telling Sheriff Clarke they were rabbit hunting. However, his description of what happened next differed from Vanderweide's. He said that after he spotted Walker, he went running down the hill. When Walker ordered him to halt, he was running too fast to stop. He ran about nine more feet, and Walker fired at him. He heard Vanderweide firing, but he couldn't remember how many shots. He saw Walker fall backward. He insisted he didn't know who it was. "When he fell, I walked up to the shaft. I looked at Walker as he lay on the dump, both as I went to the shaft and as I returned after letting down the rope. He looked apparently to be dead. I dropped the rope into the shaft so as to force whoever might be in the mine to come out the main tunnel."[36]

He admitted he did not touch or examine Walker's body to find out whether the latter were still alive. Instead, he headed back up the hill and thanked Vanderweide for saving his life. He did not know who had been shot until after they got the buggy and were heading into Durango. "I heard Callaghan say that the man killed was Joseph A. Walker. I then thought I had seen him somewhere before, but did not know where. I since learned I met him in Denver. He was then dressed in black. When at the shaft, he was in hunting clothes."[37]

He complained that when he was in Denver the previous May for the fraud investigations, he was "put in a sweat box to testify like a prisoner at the bar."[38] He denied ever being introduced to Wheeler and Hall during that visit. He said that he was in Denver for nine days and only saw Walker once and that Walker asked him a few questions.

On cross-examination, the prosecution pressed him on his reasons for going out there. He said, "I didn't know who was with Harper out there. I did not tell my wife on the morning of November third, where I was going. I kept my business secret."[39]

After Mason's testimony, the defense continued with statements from half a dozen men who had been called to the scene after the shooting. On Friday, May 1, 1908, the defense rested. Judge Pike gave his lengthy instructions to the jury, which included no less than thirty-three points to consider when rendering their decision. He told them they must either acquit the defendants or find them guilty of murder in the first degree, murder in the second degree or voluntary manslaughter. He explained in detail the differences between each charge, emphasizing that murder implied malice aforethought and manslaughter implied the absence of malice.

When the judge finished, the summations began. First, Deputy District Attorney George Lane spoke for three hours. He questioned the physical positions of the players in the drama as described by the defendants. He wondered why Mason was so callous about not checking to see if Walker was dead or alive and why they left the scene so quickly. He reminded the jury that the gunsmith Knapp had been correct in ten of twelve assessments in the gun test. He urged the jury not to dismiss Gardunio's testimony just on the basis that he was a criminal.

After Lane finished, Defense Attorney Willis A. Reese gave a two-hour summation. He accused the DA, sheriff, and U.S. officials of "staging the case,"[40] attacking their use of the dummy in the courtroom. He complained about the "gang" of government men who'd been investigating the land frauds. He insisted that the defense witnesses were more credible than Gardunio. He said Sheriff Clarke had been influenced because Clarke's cousin worked for the Department of Justice. He dismissed Agent Callaghan as "a nice boy, sort of a lady killer, but too young to be connected with the department of justice."[41] He wondered how much the gunsmith Lee Knapp had been paid for his testimony about the powder in the barrel. He said Knapp had missed on half the cases, reasoning that "four of the guns had been shot with black powder and that Knapp missed it on two of them."[42] Finally, according to the *Durango Democrat*, he appealed to the jury's personal friendship for Mason, saying: "For God's sake, if you have no consideration for Billy Mason, have some for Billy Mason's wife and daughter, and don't put him in the class with Gardunio."[43]

The *Durango Democrat* reported that this final plea "brought tears to the eyes of many in the courtroom."[44]

The following morning, a Saturday, the summations continued. Ben Russell spoke nearly three hours for the defense, and District Attorney Pulliam closed arguments. Among his many remarks, Pulliam castigated the defense for telling the jury that Knapp had been incorrect about one of the gun tests given to Knapp. He read back the stenographer's record, showing that Knapp had in fact been correct.

Finally, at 4:00 p.m., the Walker case went to the jury.

Less than five hours later, at eight twenty that evening, the jury returned with their verdict: they found both defendants not guilty.

When the verdict was read, Mrs. Emily Mason fainted.

However, this was not the end. As the defendants left the courtroom, Sheriff Clarke rearrested Mason and Vanderweide on federal charges of conspiracy to commit murder. They were escorted to a federal office where their bond was set at $10,000 each. The bonds were paid, and the two were released to their families.

On November 3, 1908, a full year after Joseph Walker was shot in the wilds of Hesperus, federal judge Robert E. Lewis made another ruling on the Walker case. He announced that the two men could be tried for conspiracy in federal court, but he set severe limits on the charges. He declared that "they may be tried for conspiracy to deprive Walker of his rights as a citizen, but evidence that they murdered him may not be introduced."[45]

Government attorneys vowed to take the case to the U.S. Supreme Court, seeking the right to charge the defendants with the murder of Walker.

Battle lines were further drawn between the federal government and La Plata County when President Teddy Roosevelt publicly referred to Agent Walker as having been assassinated.[46] On March 1, 1909, the U.S. Supreme Court began hearing arguments in the case. In early April, a year after Mason and Vanderweide were found innocent in the state district court, the U.S. Supreme Court ruled in favor of the defendants, saying they could not be put in "double jeopardy" of their lives by being tried twice for murder.

This decision was celebrated by many in the Durango area, including the *Durango Wage Earner*, which complained that a "horde of special agents still persecute them [Mason and Vanderweide]."[47]

In August 1910, nearly three years after Walker's death, officials announced that Mason and Vanderweide would be tried in federal court in Pueblo on the lesser charges of "conspiracy to interfere with a United States officer in the discharge of his duty."[48] In late October, that case was dismissed by U.S. judge Riner.

Judge Lewis's ruling in the Walker case led to a change in laws that subsequently allowed the federal government to prosecute defendants for murder. Another byproduct of the Walker case was the creation of a new federal organization that had a mandate for investigating federal crimes. It was called the Federal Bureau of Investigation.

Postscript

On November 3, 2010, a little over a century after the death of Agent Joseph Walker, his descendents and members of the Secret Service held a special

Over one hundred years after his death, Walker's descendents and the Secret Service erected this marker on his grave at Denver's Fairmount Cemetery. *Photo by Sharon Stackhouse.*

ceremony at Fairmount Cemetery in Denver, during which they unveiled a marker for Joseph Walker. Walker was the second Secret Service agent to be killed in the line of duty in the history of the agency. He was the first to be killed as the result of a homicide.

Chapter 2
Bad Blood on Bear Creek

On a cold Saturday in November 1903, neighbors found rancher Matt Luxsinger languishing in his cabin alongside Bear Creek north of Bayfield. Matt was alive but had three bullet holes in his back. He had also been beaten and nearly drowned. For the past day, he'd been lying alone in his cabin, slowly dying.

His rescuers ran for help. When authorities arrived, Matt managed to make a detailed statement about what happened. The gist of it was that a local cowboy, Jacob Zipperian, had shot him down from his horse and then dragged him to the river, where he beat and tried to drown him. During the attack, something frightened Zipperian off, at which point Luxsinger managed to hide. Zipperian returned, presumably to finish him off, but couldn't find him. Luxsinger later crawled back to his cabin, where he was discovered the next day. Investigators found marks in the dirt where Luxsinger was dragged to the river, corroborating his story.

Doctors were unable to save their gravely wounded patient, whose kidneys had been pierced by the bullets. On Saturday afternoon, thirty-seven-year-old Luxsinger died.

Zipperian was quickly captured and brought to jail in Durango. Immigrants from Germany, the Zipperian family were farmers. Twenty-three-year-old Jacob lived with his parents, Jacob and Lena, and his younger brother, Henry. Stories soon emerged that, prior to the killing, Zipperian had broken into Luxsinger's cabin, been arrested and charged with burglary. At the time of the shooting, he was out on bond.

When details of the killing came out—that Luxsinger had been shot in the back and then roped and dragged like a calf—locals were outraged. Luxsinger was popular in the area, considered "an industrious, honorable, and responsible citizen."[49]

An immigrant from Switzerland by way of Minnesota, Matt Luxsinger had previously lived as a boarder with the Sommers family, which consisted of a widow named Etta Sommers and her five children. It appeared that, at the time of the shooting, he lived alone in the cabin near Bear Creek. His parents and numerous brothers and sisters still lived in Minnesota. On Monday, November 16, 1903, Matt Luxsinger was buried in the Bayfield Cemetery. A few weeks later, members of his family arrived in town from Odessa, Minnesota, to take care of his estate.

The first week of January 1904, Jacob Zipperian went on trial for murder. District Attorney James Pulliam and Ben B. Russell prosecuted the case. Well-known local attorneys Reese McCloskey and Willis A. Reese served as his defense. Many folks from the Bear Creek–Pine River area testified at the trial. However, because there were no witnesses to the attack, the prosecution based its case primarily on Luxsinger's dying statement. The *Durango Wage Earner* summarized what Luxsinger said:

> On the morning of the 13th of November, he was about ready to leave home, to go to a neighbor's to assist in thrashing grain. The defendant rode up and told him his cattle was [sic] in defendant's field. He proceeded to the field and got them out. When he came back defendant asked him to ride up on the hill with him. He declined, and noticed that defendant held his revolver in his hand. Fearing that he intended to shoot him, he concluded that his only safety consisted in turning and running. He did so, when defendant began firing, shooting him in the back three times. He fell off his horse; the defendant came up and tied his lariet [sic] to his legs and tried to drag him towards the river. He got his knife out and cut the rope and crawled through the fence and took refuge in his grain stacks; that defendant came in the field and fastened the rope on him again and dragged him to the river and tried to drown him by putting his foot on his head and pushing it under the water; that some noise attracted his attention and he left. That when defendant had

> *gone he crawled out and hid in the brush near by. That defendant soon came back and looked all around for him but failed to find him and left again. That he afterwards crawled to his cabin three-fourths of a mile or more away where the neighbors found him the next day dying from three gunshot wounds in his back.*[50]

Because of legalities pertaining to dying declarations, the statement could not be admitted as evidence unless the prosecution proved that Luxsinger believed he was dying when he made the statement. Otherwise, it would fall into the inadmissible category of a statement by a witness who could not be cross-examined by the defense.

The prosecution, therefore, went into some detail about what went on in Luxsinger's cabin as he lay dying. Numerous friends and officials had congregated around the mortally wounded man. They testified that Luxsinger had repeatedly made comments that he was "done for." To one of his friends, he said: "Well, Reese, they've got me this time." His friend said, "Don't worry about that. You may get over this." Luxsinger replied: "No; I'll never get over this. I've got to die."[51]

The defense based their case on Zipperian's version of events, which differed considerably from Luxsinger's:

> *The defendant upon his part admitted the shooting, but excused it upon the ground of self-defense. He claimed that the meeting occurred, when, after some quarrel the dead man fired at him the ball passing into defendant's saddle. That when Luxsinger fired at him his, Luxsinger's horse, whirled about and continued to whirl around which explained the shots in the back.*[52]

The jury was out for twenty-five minutes. When they returned, they pronounced Zipperian guilty of first-degree murder. He was sentenced to life in prison.

Upon returning to his jail cell, Zipperian reportedly broke down and wept, displaying emotion for the first time. On April 30, 1904, he was received at Cañon City as prisoner number 6039.

The defense immediately filed for a new trial, which was later denied. However, his lawyers did not give up. A year later, in February 1905, the Colorado Supreme Court ruled that a section of Judge James L. Russell's instructions to the jury contained an error. According to Colorado Supreme Court records, the error lay in Judge Russell's instruction number fourteen, which included the statement:

> *Before such killing can be justified on the ground of self defense, it must appear to the reasonable satisfaction of the jury, from the whole of the evidence, that the defendant at the time of shooting had reasonable cause to believe, and did honestly believe, that the deceased was about then to kill him (the defendant) or do him some great bodily harm.*[53]

The Supreme Court ruled that this instruction was "manifestly wrong. Substantially this instruction has been condemned by this and other courts. It is not incumbent upon the defendant in a criminal case…to prove anything to the satisfaction of the jury. It is sufficient to…[raise] a reasonable doubt."[54]

Through a legal technicality, Jacob Zipperian avoided his original life sentence and served only four years for the murder. *Colorado State Archives.*

```
#6039              Jacob Zipperian
Rec                April 30th, 1904.
County             La Plata
Crime              Murder
Term               Life
Age 24             Farmer
Wtg 150            Build Medium
Htg 5, 9,          Com Florid
Eyes Blue          Hair Dark

       Marks and Scars.

Two scars on left and one over right ear.
Scar two inches long across biceps of
left arm. Vac. mark right arm. Mole on
calf of right leg, and on left side.
Wart in right armpit.
```

Record of Convict for Jacob Zipperian. *Colorado State Archives.*

Jacob Zipperian was granted a new trial. In March, Sheriff W.J. Thompson escorted Zipperian from the penitentiary at Cañon City back to jail in Durango.

The new trial began in September of 1905. Although Zipperian's previous attorneys had succeeded in getting him the second trial, the young man was now defended by a new set of lawyers: Grant E. Holderman of Longmont and Judge Miner of Denver.

Matt Luxsinger's grieving parents traveled from their home in Minnesota to attend the trial. There they sat in the courtroom and watched while their son's killer was found guilty of the lesser charge of voluntary manslaughter, with a sentence of seven to eight years in prison. This time, the jury was out for twelve hours. According to the *Durango Democrat*, "many witnesses forgot what they swore to at a former trial of this case…To sum it up briefly, the witnesses, some of them, double-crossed themselves, the court was disgusted, those who listened to the former trial disgusted, the jury was just, and we are all d——n glad that it is over."[55]

The *Silverton Standard* was a little less "d——n glad:"

> *At the first trial of this case, largely through the efforts and eloquence of Attorney B.B. Russell, of this city, who assisted in the prosecution, Zipperian received a life sentence, which he richly deserved. A more cold-blooded murder was never perpetuated than when Zipperian killed Luxsinger in a most horrible manner, and how a jury could bring in a verdict such as this last one is just a little beyond the ken of the average citizen.*[56]

On September 24, 1905, the state penitentiary once again received Jacob Zipperian, this time as prisoner number 6417. On Christmas Day 1907, after Zipperian spent a total of around four years behind bars, he was pardoned.

Postscript

Zipperian later moved to Ohio, where he worked as a streetcar motorman, married and had one child. He died in 1948.

Chapter 3
The Grave Misfortune of Kid Adams, the Ouray Highwayman

One of the old stage routes in the Ouray region was the run between the Camp Bird mine and Ouray. Sometimes called the Sneffels stage, it operated every day except Sunday. Known to carry a treasure box full of gold bullion from the Camp Bird mill, it ran without incident for a year before it proved an irresistible draw to bandits.

On Monday, October 2, 1899, the stage stopped at the mill and picked up two days' output of bullion, worth from $6,000 to $10,000 ($153,000 to $254,000, depending on how you calculate inflation.[57]) James Knowles of the Camp Bird accompanied the bullion, and a second guard, Pat Hennesey, rode behind on horseback. W.W. Almond drove the stage. As usual, they stashed the loot in an iron box beneath the driver's seat.

The stage hadn't been going long when a man jumped out from a bank of willows and pointed a Winchester at the stage driver, commanding him to put up his hands. A second man materialized in front of Hennesey's horse and ordered him to dismount. Although Hennesey had a .45 revolver hidden inside his coat, he found no opportunity to use it.

The bandits both wore slouch hats, and their clothes were smeared with dust. Black masks with large eyeholes covered their faces. They ordered the three men to lie down with their faces in the dirt. The first bandit stood guard while the second rummaged through the stage. He grabbed mail pouches and baggage but somehow failed to get the gold. It wasn't clear

Wicked Tales from Ouray, San Juan and La Plata Counties

whether he couldn't get the box opened or simply believed Almond's story that they weren't carrying any bullion that day.

The bandits told the men to get back on the stage and take off. They then stole Hennesey's horse and rode away with the mail pouch and minor items from the stage. Later, a man in the area reported that he was robbed of his horse around that time by two masked men in an excited frame of mind.

As soon as the victims reached Ouray, they called back to the Camp Bird and Revenue mines. Though everyone was relieved that nobody was hurt and the bullion was safe, posses quickly formed at the mines and headed off in pursuit. The victims had seen the bandits head in the direction of Yankee Boy Basin and the Virginius mine. Sheriff John Edgar, Under-Sheriff McQuilken and City Marshal O.C. Van Houton in Ouray also formed posses.

Camp Bird manager J.W. Benson offered a $1,000 reward for the apprehension of the bandits. Inspired by the reward, numerous miners and millworkers in the region quit work and took off in search of the robbers.

Mill at the Camp Bird Mine, shown here in 1940. The Camp Bird cranked out plenty of temptation for bandits. *Courtesy Library of Congress.*

That same evening, the Camp Bird posse located the highwaymen camped at Yankee Boy Basin. A gunfight ensued, but the bandits escaped. It was dark, and the posse pursued only briefly.

The next day, Sheriff Edgar and his men spotted the fugitives eleven miles from Ridgeway. The posse gave chase, and a running fight ensued, with both parties shooting at each other. The two bandits made for a tree-covered mountainside, but a horse stumbled and fell, dumping a bandit and his rifle. The man managed to mount again quickly and he vanished among the trees again, leaving behind a broken Winchester. He still apparently had a six-shooter. The bandits separated and disappeared.

A different version of this escape had a horse and rider making a suicidal leap into a box canyon and vanishing. This story came from the editor of the *Silverite-Plaindealer*, F.J. Hulaniski, who went into great detail describing his own heroic entry into the chase, a daring adventure during which he was pitched off his mount, making a "hasty visit to the clouds." With unabashed enthusiasm, he described his horse as a "cross between a trick mule and a Texas broncho [sic]" who "turned forward and backward summersaults [sic] with much ease, pitched in all languages, came down stiff legged like an educated steam pile-driver, and went out of one fit into another."[58]

Apparently, despite the less-than-spectacular haul of the robbery, just about every able-bodied male in the San Juans had set out to join the fun of chasing these bandits.

The *Silverite-Plaindealer* went on to describe a Tuesday night spent standing guard duty "without closing an eye or moving from the post assigned by the sheriff, who, with all the others, did likewise. The night was dark and cold, mountain lions, wolves and wild cats prowled and yelled, and taken as a whole it was no picnic."[59] In a perplexing contradiction, the *Ouray Herald* reported that on Tuesday, Edgar and his posse gave up the search and headed back down the mountain to refresh themselves with some hot supper.

Meanwhile, the stagecoach driver, W.W. Almond, also a member of some posse or other, had told authorities that he believed he recognized the voice and clothing of one of the bandits as a young man known in Ouray as "Kid Adams." He said that, prior to the robbery, Kid Adams had been hanging around the village of Sneffels (today a ghost town) with another unknown man, acting "in a very suspicious manner."[60]

On Thursday, the bandits were still scarce. Mr. Benson of the Camp Bird declared he would spare no expense in their capture, and local papers reassured their readers that the highwaymen were cornered. A chorus of voices declared that they would take the men dead or alive.

By Friday, the second bandit had been identified as Ed Perry. Before switching to stagecoach robbery, Perry had been painting the Camp Bird boardinghouse. He had also worked as a painter in Silverton and other San Juan towns. Papers reported that he was known as an OK fellow and that his partner had apparently turned him bad.

Kid Adams also went by the name of John Carter. The *Silverite-Plaindealer* described him as "young, small in stature, and an all-round tough character, desperate, unscrupulous, and possessing the nerve of a hardened pirate."[61] He had also been working at the Camp Bird as a laborer on the mine dump, a job that presumably gave him opportunity to case the area.

At some point during the next few days, Ed Perry appeared at a place called Neatherly's ranch where he ate supper and spent the night. A posse nearly nabbed him, but he heard them coming and escaped. Two ranch hands followed him to the Montrose area and notified authorities. Meanwhile, a Montrose sheriff encountered Perry at a creek where the latter was cooling his heels, literally, in the fresh mountain water. The sheriff did not arrest him, a story that inspired much irate grumbling among Montrose citizens. When the sheriff returned later with reinforcements, Perry had gone. The Montrose sheriff's department later defended themselves, saying the sheriff did not know who Perry was when he first encountered him.

By Saturday, the reported value of the gold that the robbers overlooked had nearly doubled.

That same day, the saga turned much more serious. Deputy Sheriff George Kinchen of San Miguel County wired Sheriff Edgar, asking him about the reward and requesting an arrest warrant for Adams. Several days later, he sent the following wire: "I have killed John Carter [Kid Adams], will be in Placerville tomorrow morning with the body—answer if I shall ship remains to Ouray."[62]

Before taking his last breath, the Kid had told Kinchen his name was John Carter and that his parents lived in Texas. The story later emerged that he wasn't John Carter from Texas but Walter Adams from a local family. His father was identified as the late James S. Adams, a prominent cattleman who had run a ranch located between Montrose and Delta.

After some delay, the body finally arrived in Ouray. Newspapers reported gruesome details about the condition of the Kid—that he was "shot clear through the middle of the body, and the whole top of the head is shot away by a revolver ball."[63] Deputy Kinchen described what happened for several reporters. He said he learned that the Kid had been spotted heading down Disappointment Creek in San Miguel County. Kinchen followed that trail to Jim Mairs's cattle ranch on lower Disappointment, which is where he found him, apparently working with Mairs.

Kinchen approached the ranch house and chatted with the men, pretending to be looking to buy some cattle. Mairs invited him in for supper and to spend the night. The Kid was watching him closely and Kinchen noted that he was armed.

At some point, Kinchen confided his intentions to one of the other men. Around ten o'clock at night, he judged the time right, pulled his gun on the Kid and told him to surrender. The Kid jumped away and pulled his gun, and the two men began firing at each other. During the gunfight, Kinchen and the other two men fled the cabin, leaving the Kid alone inside. Half an hour later, the men outside heard a shot.

They waited until the next morning before entering, when they discovered the Kid had shot himself in the head.

The coroner held an inquest and officially confirmed Kinchen's story.

Despite the coroner's ruling, rumors soon circulated that Kinchen had murdered the Kid in cold blood. Folks complained that Walter Adams was only twenty-one years old and from a respected Colorado family. The *Aspen Tribune* also reported Undertaker James Pierson of Ouray as saying, "I have given the cause of death, murder. This is my privilege. The Kid didn't get any money; neither did he kill anyone and he was shot in the back. His hair was not burned by powder. He did wrong but he should have been taken to Cañon City alive instead of dead."[64]

Dr. Hamilton Fish, who examined the body, said that a piece of the brain and skull were missing and attributed this to an autopsy, though no autopsy had been held. The *Aspen Tribune* reported a rumor that someone had tampered with the body to conceal the fact that his skull had been crushed, though it wasn't clear why someone would do that.

Kinchen admitted that his bullet had hit the Kid in the back and come out the stomach. He responded to the attacks with this indignant offer: "Who dares say I killed the Kid in cold blood? He can meet me at any time with any weapon and have it out."[65]

Kinchen did have his supporters; some insisted that the Kid was a "tough character" and would have killed Kinchen if he could. In Ouray, according to the *Silverite-Plaindealer*, "Some irresponsible idiot went so far this week as to post a notice on a telegraph pole near the post office offering '$1,000 reward for the scalp' of Mr. Benson and $1500 reward for Deputy Kinchen, dead or alive. Marshal Van Houten very properly tore it down."[66]

Either way, Kinchen collected his reward and quickly left town.

A couple months later, a *Telluride Journal* reporter said he had spoken to a man who was in the Disappointment cabin at the time of the shooting. The unnamed man told the reporter that it was the "merest accident that Adams didn't get the deputy" and that Adams fired first.[67] Adams had also apparently boasted about robbing the Union Pacific the previous summer and that he had shot a Wyoming sheriff.

On Saturday night, October 14, 1899, twelve days after the robbery, the stepmother of Kid Adams, Mrs. Lucy Adams Whipple, arrived in Ouray to take charge of the remains. Walter's mother, Emma Frazier Adams, had died when he was very young, and his father had remarried when Walter was seven. The father, James Adams, had died a few years earlier, and Lucy kept in her care the remaining Adams children, two of whom were hers. In June 1898, Lucy Adams married Don Whipple.

Apparently overcome with grief over the death of her stepson, she described him as a "reckless, good-hearted fellow, with a dare-devil disposition, and has never been in serious trouble but once before." She admitted he held up a stage in March 1898 at Meeker in Routt County. Drunk at the time, Walter made the driver dance and sing and drink whiskey before Walter took off empty-handed, having made no attempt to actually rob the stage. Authorities arrested him but let him go because he was so young.

Lucy Whipple took his remains to Cañon City where one of his relatives was a retired Baptist preacher. Walter was buried beside his parents.

While all this was going on, another young man of quite a different sort involved himself in the Kid Adams story. Dr. Alexander J. McIvor-Tyndall, dubbed the "highest authority on the science" of palm reading and author of an upcoming book on the subject, had been giving private readings in Room 24 at Ouray's Beaumont Hotel.[68] He was described by an enthusiastic Ouray reporter as "a man of superlative intelligence, a bright conversationalist, and a deep thinker on scientific subjects."[69]

The *Silverite-Plaindealer* hired McIvor-Tyndall to do a reading on Kid Adams. The palmist took an impression from the dead man's hand, which was printed in large form on the front page of the paper. The scientist first offered several remarks about the shape of Walter's nose, forehead and earlobes, which apparently indicated that he was a desperado. As for Walter's palm, "the head line…is short, erratic, crooked, and indirect. It is much like the head line of a natural lunatic."[70] Dr. McIvor-Tyndall went on to make a dire prediction about the late Walter Adams's fate: "A distorted and intense imagination, a misdirected ambition and an unreasoning will are the prominent features of this hand. But the unfortunate position of the lines of life, head, and heart presage grave misfortune."[71]

There were no further notices about the fate of the other robber, Ed Perry.

Chapter 4
Dangerous Women

THE DISAPPEARANCE OF MAX DALLAVALLE

Local newspapers took no notice when thirty-one-year-old Max Dallavalle of Silverton went missing. After a few days, friends and coworkers from the Alta mine went looking for him at the small Dallavalle home at the corner of Cement and Fourteenth Streets. His wife, Rosa, told them he had gone to Oregon.

The Dallavalles, who sometimes shortened their name to Dalla, were no strangers to trouble. Although they had two living children, Stephana and Raymond, three other children had died as infants, and they lost their daughter, Eunice, when she was only five months old. Newspaper reports said they had previously lived in Durango, where the family was split apart when Rosa left Max for another man. Rosa and her new paramour moved to Silverton, where the latter soon died of pneumonia. A short time later, Max and Rosa reconciled. They stayed in Silverton, and Max found work at the Alta mine.

Max Dallavalle disappeared in mid-September 1911. A week or so later, Mrs. Dallavalle moved into another house with an Austrian immigrant named Victor Pangranzi. Pangranzi worked at the Silverton Dairy and had apparently been boarding with the Dallavalles. Three months later, in December 1911, Rosa Dallavalle packed up her children and moved to California with Victor Pangranzi.

About seven months later, on Monday, July 22, 1912, two men discovered a skeleton at the base of Kendall Mountain, near the mouth of today's Swansea Gulch, close to the Lackawanna mine.

The men contacted authorities, and Coroner R.E. McLeod headed to the scene. The skeleton had suffered considerable predation, but the coroner was able to locate the head and other missing parts. He determined that the man had been shot and his body partially burned. No gun was present, so the coroner ruled out suicide. A thick piece of rope found nearby indicated that the man had probably been killed elsewhere and dragged by rope to the spot.

Among the clothing, they found a bill for groceries dated June 1911 from Cascade Grocery Company in Ouray. The bill was addressed to Max Dallavalle.

Authorities searched the original Dallavalle house but found it had been scrubbed clean.

At the coroner's inquest, Dr. J.S. Fox confirmed that the skeleton was Max Dallavalle. He said that the skeleton possessed the same unusual deformity he had seen on Max—a bone growth on the hip.

A young girl named May McCloskey, who lived near the Dallavalles, testified that on the night of September 15, 1911, she was awakened by two gunshots. She got up and heard two men arguing at the Dallavalle house. She heard and saw the flash of a third shot fired by one of the men.

Another neighbor, Mrs. Arietta, also testified about hearing the shots. She said she also saw Victor Pangranzi throw a bundle of clothing into the Animas River the following morning. Later that day, she saw Pangranzi head off on his horse in the direction of the spot where the skeleton was found.

After several others testified, the coroner ruled that "Max Dallavalle came to his death on or about September 15, 1911, from the result of gunshot wounds or knife wounds, inflicted on him by Victor Pangranzi with felonious intent. Said Victor Pangranzi being then and there aided, assisted and abetted by Mrs. Max Dallavalle."[72]

It was then left to law enforcement to track down the suspects. Charles Thompson, the proprietor of the Silverton Dairy, offered up a handy clue. About six weeks earlier, he had received a letter from Pangranzi, asking if he could return to Silverton and get his old job back at the dairy. The letter was written from Jamestown, California. Silverton authorities immediately wired law enforcement in Jamestown to be on the lookout for the couple.

California authorities soon reported that Pangranzi had gone to Wallace, Idaho, sans Mrs. Dallavalle. A flurry of telegrams ensued between agencies, and Idaho lawmen soon identified and arrested Pangranzi, who was now using a false name. Under questioning, Pangranzi admitted his real name but denied knowing anything about the murder. He said he had simply been rooming with Rosa Dallavalle, who told him her husband had gone to Trinidad.

Silverton coroner McLeod traveled to Idaho and brought Pangranzi back to face charges. Meanwhile, Mrs. Dallavalle was arrested by Sheriff Kramer (or Traner) of Sonora, California, near Jamestown, who escorted her to Silverton.

Officers announced that they had found letters in Pangranzi's possession from Rosa Dallavalle that pointed at their guilt. By the time of his preliminary hearing a week later, Pangranzi had confessed to the crime:

> *I think it was either the 15th or the 16th of September, 1911, about 1 o'clock that I shot Dalladalle [sic] who was angry. It was very dark and I got my gun. Afterwards I shot him four times and he fell dead in the room. Mrs. Dalladalle [sic] was there and we expected the police to come at once so we put the body under the bed and wrapped it in a blanket. The woman wanted to burn him so we poured some turpentine over him and piled brush wood about the body and set it on fire.*[73]

A few days after Pangranzi's confession, the case grew more complicated. Rosa Dallavalle insisted that she, not Pangranzi, killed her husband.

In late September 1912, a year after Dallavalle's death, both Rosa Dallavalle and Victor Pangranzi went on trial for murder. The presiding judge was Charles A. Pike. The defense attorney was Cyril Dunn, who had only been admitted to the bar a few months earlier. The chief witnesses for the prosecution were May McCloskey and Anna Sullivan. Both young ladies testified that they "heard three shots and they saw two men in the Dallavalle yard."[74]

Taking the stand in her own defense, Rosa Dallavalle told a story that cast the case in a different light than what had previously appeared in the papers. She testified that she had married Max Dallavalle back in Austria and come to America five years earlier. Shortly after their marriage, Dallavalle began abusing her. He frequented saloons and bordellos and forced her to work in order to feed their children. She said that, on one occasion, he threatened to kill their son. On the night of the murder, Max came home angry and threatening to kill her if she didn't give him whatever money she had. He rifled through a trunk owned by Pangranzi, took ten dollars from it and left the house. When Pangranzi came home, she told him what her husband had done. Pangranzi then went to his trunk and brought out a revolver, hiding it so Max couldn't find it. Max returned in the early hours of the morning, entered his wife's bedroom and threatened her with a knife, saying, "This is your last night, I want to wash my hands in your blood."[75] She escaped from him, ran to Pangranzi's room and found the revolver. As Max followed her in, she shot him. She then tried to turn the gun on herself, but Victor wrestled the gun away from her.

Victor Pangranzi also took the stand. He continued to claim that he had shot Max in order to protect Rosa.

Also testifying was Charles Thompson of the Silverton Dairy, for whom Pangranzi had worked. He said that Pangranzi had been one of his best employees and he had no trouble with him until Mrs. Dallavalle "began coming around his place."[76]

At 9:35 p.m. on Tuesday, the jury retired to deliberate. Wednesday at 10:30 a.m., they returned with their verdict. The testimony from Victor and Rosa had apparently been convincing: they found Victor Pangranzi guilty of the lesser charge of voluntary manslaughter, and they acquitted Rosa Dallavalle.

Victor Pangranzi was sentenced to one to eight years in the penitentiary, and he was received at Cañon City on October 2, 1912. About three years later, January 2, 1916, he was released on parole. His sentence was discharged six months later. Pangranzi's prison records identify Rosa Dallavalle of Silverton, Colorado, as his common-law wife.

Max Dallavalle was buried in Silverton's Hillside Cemetery, near his five-month-old daughter, Eunice.

Attack in the Night

In the early hours on a Monday morning in May 1912, Dr. W.C. DuBois was awakened by frantic men from the Salabar Ranch near Ignacio. They told him one of the ranch hands, Martine Atencio, was in desperate trouble and needed help. Martine was a highly respected citizen of the community and had lived in the area for a long time.

Dr. DuBois rushed through the night to the small Atencio ranch house on Ute Creek, three miles east of Ignacio. There he found Mrs. Bernardina Atencio and the five young Atencio children. Husband and father Martine lay in bed, barely alive with an extreme wound to his head.

Bernardina explained that Martine had come home from work earlier that day with the injury, saying he had been kicked by a horse. The doctor examined the wound. Martine's head was so mangled that DuBois doubted the man could have walked back from the Salabar ranch, where the accident supposedly happened. The injury did not look like it came from a horse.

A few hours later, at eight o'clock in the morning, Martine Atencio died. Still skeptical of Mrs. Atencio's story, Dr. DuBois called authorities.

Sheriff Tim McCluer arrived from Durango, along with Coroner Hood, Attorney George Lane and a man named Sam Ethridge. They took one look at Martine's head and agreed with the doctor that Martine had not been kicked by a horse. A quick search of the area around the ranch house revealed a blood-spattered ax. The men concluded that it had been used to smash Martine's head.

They sat Bernardina Atencio down and began to ask questions. Her story about the horse soon fell apart, and her explanations grew increasingly muddled. It wasn't long before the truth emerged:

The night before as Martine drifted to sleep, Bernardina slipped out of bed, crept across the floor and stepped out the front door into the night.

There, her paramour, Juan Garcia, waited for her in the darkness. She told Juan that her husband was not quite asleep.

She went back into the house, leaving the front door unlocked.

Later, between nine and ten o'clock at night, Garcia crept into the house, carrying the ax. He stepped quietly into the bedroom and stood over the sleeping Martine. Then he lifted the ax and swung it down on the prone figure, smashing the skull. Atencio rolled off the bed from the blow, and Garcia struck him again before escaping into the night.

After Bernardina's confession, the sheriff and his men headed out to a ranch on Spring Creek about two miles away. There they located Garcia and arrested him. For unexplained reasons, they also arrested Garcia's father and two brothers.

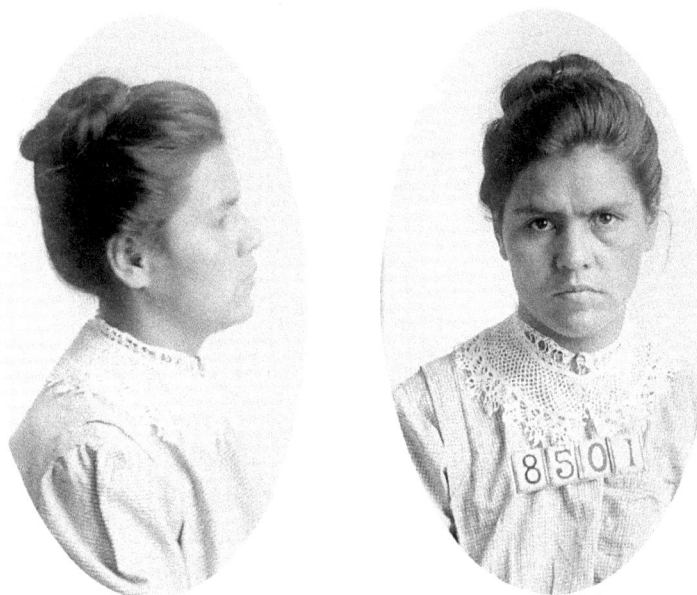

This mug shot of a cranky-looking Bernardina Atencio includes a mysterious picture of a man at her throat—perhaps a cameo or a button. *Colorado State Archives.*

```
8501 - ATENCIO
Received, June 29, 1912.
County, LaPlata;
Crime, Murder;
Sentence 1 2/3 to 2 years;
occupation, house-wife;
sex - female;
age, 24; weight, 125; height, 4-8; complexion, dark;
nationality, Mexican; build, short and small;
hair, black; eyes, black;

                    Marks and Scars;

Teeth perfect;   No scars on body or head;
```

Bernardina's Record of Convict. *Colorado State Archives.*

Wicked Tales from Ouray, San Juan and La Plata Counties

Though he killed her husband for her, Juan Garcia does not appear to be the man in Bernardina's cameo. *Colorado State Archives.*

```
8481-GARCIA.
Recd.6-16-12.
County,La Plata.
Crime,Murder.
Sentence,Life.
Occupation,Laborer.
Age 39.Weight134.Height5-4.Complexion,Dark.Hair black.
Eyes brown.Build short-light.Nationality,Mexican.
Bust 34.Waist 31.Thigh.17 1/2.Neck 13.1/2.Hat 7.Shoes7.

              MARKS & SCARS.

White spot in hair.Scar back of head.Pock marked.
Good teeth.Scar back of left shoulder.Hairy arms,legs
and chest.
```

Juan's Record of Convict. *Colorado State Archives.*

Juan Garcia confessed that he and Bernardina had been having a relationship since the previous March, and the two had planned the murder for a month.

In early June, Juan Garcia and Bernardina Atencio appeared before Judge Pike in district court in Durango. Garcia pleaded guilty to first-degree murder. Bernardina pleaded not guilty to the same charge.

Garcia was quickly sentenced to life in prison. Bernardina was found guilty of being accessory during the fact, was fined $500 and sentenced to two years in prison.

The five young Atencio children were taken in by neighboring families. On June 16, 1912, Juan Garcia arrived at Cañon City to begin serving his sentence. He left behind a wife in Ignacio, Nasaria Garcia. On September 6, 1933, after he served twenty-one years, he was released on parole.

Bernardina Atencio was sent to Cañon City on June 29, 1912. A year and a half later, on December 19, 1913, she was released on parole. Her sentence was discharged March 19, 1914.

The Body in the Well

On a warm August day in 1919, in the rural settlement of La Posta, south of Durango, the body of a man was found in an abandoned well.

The body hadn't been there long, and authorities quickly determined that the dead man was Mercurio Vallejos, a popular local man. Mercurio lived with his eighteen-year-old wife, Lucia, and their two-year-old son in La Posta, at the intersection of today's Colorado Road 213 and Willimax Lane.

Mercurio had fought with the U.S. armed forces in World War I. When the war ended, he returned home, bringing along his twenty-two-year-old nephew, Francisco "Frank" Vallejos, a Mexican national.

Francisco immediately became overly attentive to Lucia. His interest soon became so obvious that Mercurio told Francisco to get lost and forbade him from coming around the house. However, Lucia apparently returned the nephew's affection. While Mercurio was out working in the fields, Francisco and Lucia continued to meet secretly.

As soon as Mercurio's body was identified, authorities interviewed Lucia Vallejos. She confessed that Francisco had, on the night of August 19, attacked

Wicked Tales from Ouray, San Juan and La Plata Counties

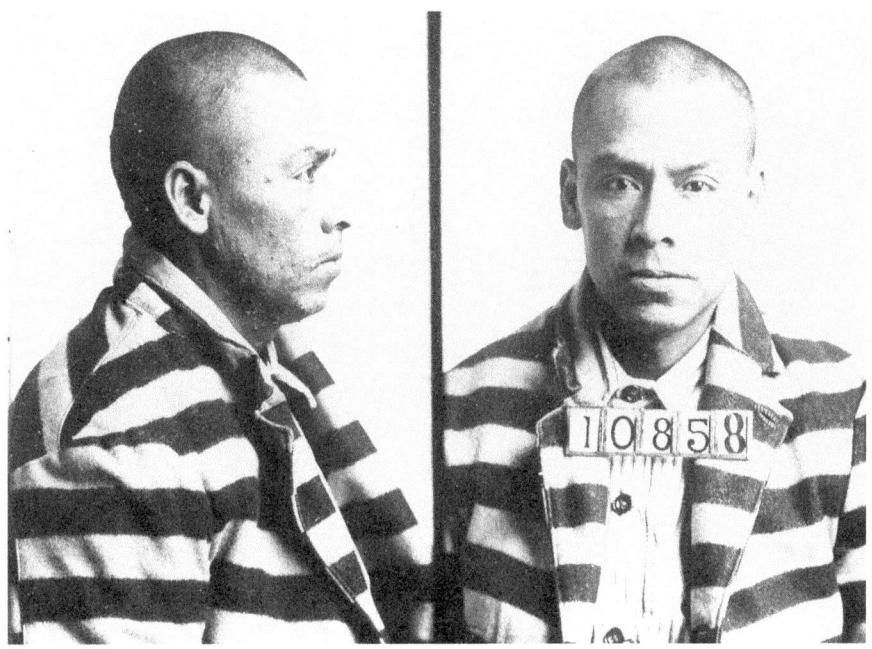

Francisco Vallejos served seven years of a life sentence for his first-degree murder conviction. *Colorado State Archives.*

```
Francisco Vallejos. No. 10858. Rec'd Dec 1st, 1919.
From La Plata County. Life for Murder. Age 22.
Weight 135. Height 5.4,3/4. Complexion Dark. Bust
36. Waist 31. Thigh 17. Neck 14½. Hat 6.7/8.
Shoes 5½. Hair Black. Eyes Dk-brown. Build Med.
Born in Mexico. Nationality Mexican. Occupation
Common Laborer.
Marks and Scars:- Scar front of head. Scar right
corner of mouth. Teeth Good. Scar front near Right
armpit. Small scar above left elbow. Scars on left
knee-cap. Scar above left groin. White mark above
right groin. Dark mark on left side near waist line.
Scar on right side of back. near waist line.
Relatives:
Emidio Vasquez    (Parents) Ecuandurejo, Mexico.
                     62 Main Street.



      Finger Print Class'n  ------------
```

Francisco's Record of Convict. *Colorado State Archives.*

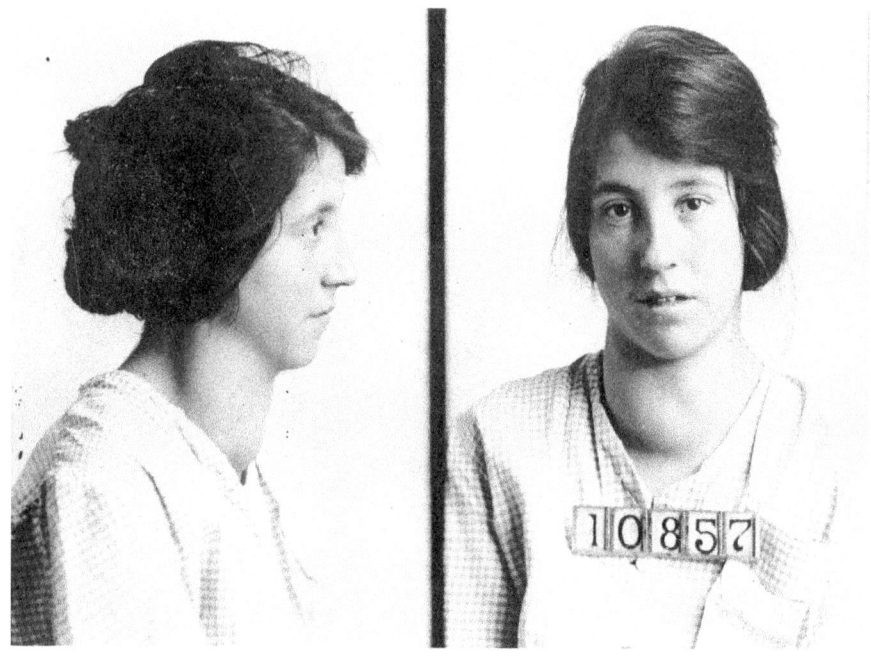

Lucia Vallejos was only eighteen when she went to prison. *Colorado State Archives.*

```
Lucia Vallejos No. 10857.  Rec'd Dec. 1st,.1919.
From La Plata County. 12 to 17 yrs, for Murder.
Age 19.  Weight 116. Height 5.4,½.  Complexion
Dark.  Bust 35.  Waist 28.  Thigh 22.  Neck 15.
Shoes 5.  Hair Dk-brown.  Eyes Brown.  Build Slight
Born in Cortez,Colo. Nationality Amer-Mex.  Occu-
pation House-keeper.
Marks and Scars:- Large goitre on neck.  Scar on
right elbow.
Relatives:
  Doloritas Lucero (Mo) Posta, Colo.
  Frank Lucero (Fa)    Posta, Colo.
  Marcizo Lucero (Bro) San Francisco, Calif,.


     Finger Print Class'n  --------------
```

Lucia's Record of Convict. *Colorado State Archives.*

his uncle with the butt of a revolver and the handle of a sledgehammer. The beating was severe, and Mercurio died. The murder was reportedly witnessed by the Vallejoses' son. Francisco then somehow carried Mercurio's body out to the abandoned well a half mile away and dumped it into the depths.

The coroner's inquest ruled that Mercurio had been murdered at the hands of Francisco and Lucia, and both were hauled off to jail in Durango. Neither of the pair was present in the courtroom during the inquest, as many residents of La Posta were friends of Mercurio, and threats had been made against the defendants.

Two weeks after the murder, both Francisco and Lucia entered not guilty pleas in Durango district court. Local attorneys Barry Sullivan and James Pulliam represented the pair, neither of whom could read or write. Bail was denied, and the defendants were returned to county jail until they could be tried during the next court term.

In a nearly two-week trial, the pair was tried together for murder. Like the Atencio case, their trial received scant coverage in the press. Furthermore, newspapers consistently used the incorrect spelling of "Ballegos." On August 29, 1919, the *Ignacio Chieftain* gave a brief rundown of the case and announced that the jury was out for only thirty minutes before returning with a verdict. They found Francisco guilty of first-degree murder and Lucia guilty of second-degree murder as an accessory. The prosecution's case rested largely on Lucia's confession.

Judge William N. Searcy sentenced Francisco Vallejos to life in prison. He was received at Cañon City on December 1, 1919. In May 1926, his sentence was commuted by Governor Morley for deportation. On November 1926, after serving seven years, he was released on parole and presumably deported.

Lucia Vallejos was sentenced to twelve to seventeen years. In April 1926, also after serving seven years, she was released on parole. Her sentence was discharged on October 3, 1928.

Chapter 5
Durango Desperadoes
Porter and Ike Stockton

Not every gunslinger of the Old West landed in the pages of books and magazines and earned a lasting reputation. However, among the many trigger-happy malcontents who roamed the lawless frontier, there were a few who possessed a little something extra—perhaps it was charm or charisma, a gift of salesmanship or just enough humanity to make folks trust them. Whatever it was, some killers had loyal advocates among the citizenry. Some even managed to get themselves hired as lawmen by anxious residents of remote and unprotected towns.

Such a pair was Porter and Ike Stockton.

Census records show that the Stockton brothers were born in Upshur, Texas, though one biographer named Cleburne as their town of origin. Most historians say Ike was the older of the two, but the census shows that Ike, or Isaac, was the younger brother, born February 29, 1852. Porter was born in 1850.

The brothers spent their early years in Texas, Kansas and New Mexico. Their names appear in some accounts of the range wars that waged in New Mexico during the 1870s, including the Lincoln County War and Colfax County War. While still in Texas, the brothers married two half sisters. In 1870, Port married Emily Jane Cowan, and the couple had three daughters: Sarah, Mary and Carrie "Essie May". In 1873, Isaac married Amanda Ellen Robinson, Emily Cowan's half sister by the same mother. Their daughter, Delilah, was born in 1875; son Guy was born 1880.

Accounts vary about which of the brothers was wilder. A couple things were clear: Port Stockton had a reputation for shooting men, and Ike Stockton showed a fanatical devotion to his brother.

William Porter "Port" Stockton's name first popped up in Colorado in 1873 when he was involved in a brawl in Trinidad, during which a friend of his was killed. Port later went looking for the shooter and killed another man by mistake.[77] He apparently faced no repercussions for this killing. In Cimmaron, New Mexico, in 1876, he killed a man named Juan Gonzales who objected to Stockton's attentions to his wife. A posse captured Stockton and threw him in jail. When brother Ike found out about the arrest, he showed up at the Cimmaron jail, pulled a gun on the jailer and demanded his brother's release. According to Ike's biographer, this process was repeated when Porter was again arrested, thrown in jail and "rescued" at gunpoint by Ike.

In June 1879, a liveryman named Ed Withers was shot and killed in Otero, New Mexico. Some reports were vague about who the shooter was, but the *Denver Republican* identified the killer as Porter Stockton.[78]

During the late 1870s, the Stocktons lingered in the San Juan area, particularly Durango and Animas City. There they busied themselves primarily with cattle rustling. Among their cohorts was another pair of brothers from Durango, Dyson and Harg (or Hargo or Argo) Eskridge. Another hanger-on was a young man who would prove to have a significant impact on Ike Stockton's life—his name was Bert Wilkinson.

In early 1880, despite his reputation as a cattle rustler, Port Stockton became marshal of Animas City. Today absorbed by the city of Durango, Animas City at that time was a bustling outpost of several hundred citizens. Marshal Stockton quickly gained a reputation for being bad tempered and quick on the trigger.

Animas City had a law against firearms. In July 1880, a man called Captain Hart came into town with a revolver on hand. Marshal Stockton ordered him to give up the weapon. Hart exchanged words with Stockton, and the latter shot Hart in the cheek. Luckily, Hart survived the encounter.[79] A few eyebrows in town were raised over this incident, but it wasn't clear who was at fault, so nothing came of it.

Stockton's character became clearer one day the following September when he entered a barbershop for a shave. The barber, J.W. Allen, reported to be an educated and well-traveled Māori, was apparently nervous and nicked his customer. Stockton pulled his gun and shot at the barber, the bullet grazing the back of the man's head. He then pistol-whipped him.

This time, the citizens of Animas City were outraged. The mayor, Eugene Engley, deputized another man, and together they arrested Stockton. Inexplicably, they allowed Stockton to keep his weapon and let him go for supper. (Some accounts say he went home to his wife to eat; others say he went to P.J. Cate's hotel.) At some point during the meal, despite being guarded, Stockton slipped out a window, robbed a local man of his horse and made his escape.

Stockton returned to New Mexico where he apparently filed or already had a homestead. On Christmas Eve 1880, several friends of the Stocktons decided to crash a Christmas party being given at the Francis M. Hamblet ranch in northern New Mexico. (Hamblet later moved to the Durango area.) Annoyed at not being invited, the men showed up drunk and rowdy. Accounts vary as to who the men were, but most agree that two of the party crashers were James Garrett and Dyson Eskridge, associates of Porter Stockton. Some say that Port was with them. After disgusting the ladies at the party with their behavior, the men were asked to leave. They complied but soon returned and fired shots at the house. A man named George Brown was killed; also shot was a man named Oscar Pruett, who later died. Some accounts say Pruett was a friend of Stockton's and was among the party crashers; others say he was at the party and was shot by the Stockton group.

On the run, Eskridge and Garrett headed for Port Stockton's home near Flora Vista, northeast of Farmington, New Mexico. An irate posse followed them there, and on January 4, 1881, they engaged in a gun battle with the people inside the house. During this fight, Port Stockton was shot dead. Porter's wife, Emily, was also involved in the gun battle; she was injured when her Winchester rifle was shot out of her hands.

The death of Port Stockton apparently roused his brother, Ike, from the slumber of a reasonably normal life in Animas City. Ike embarked on a private war that lasted throughout most of 1881. He traveled to New Mexico and tried unsuccessfully to get his brother's killers arrested. He took Emily and her three children back to Animas City. Then he called upon friends to help him wreak vengeance on his brother's killers. These friends included the Eskridge brothers, Harg and Dyson Eskridge. Rumors soon ran wild, with newspapers reporting that the desperadoes were stealing cattle and killing cowboys. The gang's "territory" ranged between Port's New Mexico homestead and Durango. They reportedly stole thirty-five cattle out of New Mexico and drove them to Durango, where they sold them. The victims of these thefts were the men from the Farmington area who were involved in the shooting of Port Stockton.

In April, a large group of citizens petitioned New Mexico governor Lewis Wallace to do something about the Ike Stockton gang. They asked for

> *prompt action against the desperadoes who disgrace the territory. On March 29, Governor Wallace ordered Adjutant-General Frost to go immediately with sixty stand of rifles and ten thousand rounds of ammunition and organize two infantry companies to act as sheriff's posse. The robbers are led by Ike Stockton and have headquarters near the Colorado line at Durango.*[80]

On April 15, 1881, the *Leadville Daily Herald* reported that "Durango is in a state of anarchy owing to the depredations of the Stockton gang."[81]

Perhaps getting no satisfaction from the government, the Farmington men formed a posse and burned the Port Stockton ranch house. They drove Ike and his buddies out of the area, but the latter soon returned. The gang was camped on the burned-out property when two of the opposing party approached. This led to a gun battle during which Ike shot and killed one of the men, Aaron Barker. This shooting put Ike on the wanted outlaw list, and he fled back to Colorado.

The Farmington men followed him to Durango, arriving on April 11, 1881. From there, they went to Animas City where Ike had a ranch. The New Mexicans quickly realized that Ike had too many friends in the area, so turned around and headed back toward home. As they traveled past Durango, members of Ike's gang fired at them, which started an hourlong gun battle, during which two bystanders were wounded. Citizens of Durango considered themselves under attack from the Farmington men, and reports appeared in the paper about bullet holes in many buildings in town. The *Dolores News*, a pro-Stockton paper, wrote:

> *The Farmington people have made a grave mistake in attacking this town, firing in among residences containing women and children, and endangering the lives of people who have no part in their quarrels. There is a legal way*

> *of making arrests, and the people of Durango will not permit men to come into this town to take them in any other way, especially a band of men who have shown the reckless disposition manifested by this party.*[82]

This private war continued to fill the local newspapers with stories and rumors, nearly all contradicting each other. Finally, Ike left Durango and headed for Rico. There he was fortunate to have gained the friendship of the editors of the *Dolores News*: Chas. Jones and Frank Hartman. In the coming months, these men would become Ike's most vocal advocates. The 1880 census for Rico shows printers Chas. Jones and Frank Hartman sharing a household with "Argo" Harg Eskridge and B.W. "Bert" Wilkinson, both compatriots of Ike Stockton.

Meanwhile rewards were offered in New Mexico for members of the gang. Still in Rico, Stockton and Eskridge boldly wrote letters to the governors of New Mexico and Colorado, denying all charges against them and explaining why they would not turn themselves in to the New Mexicans: "We claim that we are respectable, law-abiding citizens and have always been so, but we need not explain to you at length the danger to which we would be subjected should we permit ourselves to be placed unarmed and unprotected in an insecure country."[83]

Ike offered to surrender, as long as he and his colleagues were given protection and guaranteed safety, provided the trial wouldn't be held in Rio Arriba County, New Mexico, and that it would be done in secret and at an undisclosed location.

This offer was not accepted.

New Mexican authorities were hoping that Colorado authorities would arrest Stockton and hand him over, but time passed and he wasn't arrested. When New Mexican papers complained about this, the *Dolores News* again defended Stockton and his men: "Suffice it to say that every citizen of southwestern Colorado, who is correctly informed upon the troubles of last winter, are sympathizers with the men who compose the so-called Eskridge-Stockton gang. This is true merely because they have conducted themselves at all times and in all places as gentlemen."[84]

The paper also wrote about injuries that Emily Stockton had suffered during the gun battle that killed her husband, Porter:

> She is now a cripple for life, suffering the tortures of hell. One shot fired at her passed through the right hand and on through the left arm, paralyzing that limb, and rendering both limbs useless. Another shot entered the lower part of the left breast, ranging downward into the left side, where it is now lodged. This unfortunate woman has left to her support, three helpless children. Mrs. Stockton is destitute of any means of support, except the aid she will receive at the hands of Ike Stockton the surviving brother. It is reliably stated that the men who killed Port Stockton strictly forbade any of the neighboring women to go to the aid of Mrs. Stockton.[85]

In May, New Mexico governor Wallace offered a $500 reward for Ike Stockton and $250 each for members of his gang, including Harg Eskridge. The *Dolores News* was still defending the men dubbed by other newspapers as the "Durango Desperadoes": "On looking over the events of this disastrous trouble we find no action in which the persons mentioned have not been in the right, absolutely and entirely."[86]

Although the *Dolores News* took on the role of principal advocate for Ike Stockton, despite mounting evidence that he wasn't such a good fellow, other newspapers also defended him. Stockton clearly possessed a charisma that charmed many of those who met him, including this reporter from the *Ouray Times*:

> He has no ruffian style. You would not notice anything wild about him, only his restless eyes which seem to be continually glancing here and there. He is a little smaller than the medium size of men, walks briskly, slightly stooped. Dresses well—wears a white shirt, black suit, stiff hat, and a neatly fitting boot. Dark hair, cut short, is dark complexioned, sharp features, slight beard, eyes small and piercing. He has a clear, feminine, ringing voice, and when talking is quite sociable and entertaining. I have studied him closely and see nothing which would indicate a desperate character.[87]

This same writer also had interesting comments about Eskridge (without saying whether it was Harg or Dyson):

> He is a tall, raw-boned young man, with a fine black moustache, heavy jaw-bone and large, prominent chin. His lips are firmly set together, only

speaking when spoken to, seldom laughs or speaks aloud. He dresses more after the cow-boy style, walks slowly with his head down, and one hand in his coat-pocket. He seems to notice everything. When turning into a street he looks quickly up and down, takes a sly glance back of him, and then passes on as if he expected to meet the enemy at any time. And in case he should, he is always prepared. He is the crack shot of the gang. Just what his past record is I can't say. But he seems to be more cold-blooded and naturally desperate than any of them. He does not command the respect Stockton does. He has made some "gun plays" and "bad breaks" here.[88]

The writer then describes an episode where Eskridge interrupted a wedding in the home of a Farmington man named Coe and nearly killed a fellow he had mistaken for someone he didn't like. There was another incident where Eskridge shot his gun into the street to make a man "dance" because the latter had expressed support for the Coes.[89]

In late May, reports came that Harg Eskridge had shot a fellow known as Jim "Kid" White who reportedly was scheming to capture Eskridge for the reward. White later died in the hospital. There are no records of Eskridge being arrested or serving a prison sentence for this killing.

Also in May 1881, a man named J.W. Lacy was murdered. According to the *Dolores News*, Lacy was married to a cousin of the Stocktons, was a close friend of Ike's and Ike managed Lacy's herd of cattle. The paper reported that Lacy had been killed by a man named Dan Howland "because he was Ike Stockton's friend," as they announced in a headline on May 28, 1881. The story presented by the *Dolores News* was that the "Farmington mob" wanted to break up the friendship between Lacy and Stockton, so they sent Lacy anonymous letters saying that Stockton had been stealing his cattle. Lacy investigated and found this to be untrue. Then his wife began receiving mysterious letters, saying that Stockton was planning to kill Lacy. Then, according to the *Dolores News*, Dan Howland murdered Lacy in cold blood, presumably at the behest of the Farmington people. Chances are that a few details are missing from this version of events. The only further mention of it was a notice in the *Dolores News* on June 4 that the New Mexico ranchers were "harboring Dan Howland in their midst."[90]

In June, the *Dolores News* complained that they'd been

accused of the terrible crime of being the "organ of the Stockton-Eskridge party." Yes, and we are thankful that it is in our power to rectify some of the malicious lies which have been circulated about them. It is the heaven-born privilege of a newspaper to correct error, and we thank the stars that shine in a San Juan sky that our vertebral column is stiff enough to undertake this case, in the face of intimidation and threats and the entire outside newspaper fraternity to buck against.[91]

That month, a brief "Indian war" erupted between white settlers and Paiutes in Utah. Stockton and Eskridge and other members of the gang joined the fight and gained for themselves considerable praise in the press. Harg Eskridge, after first being reported killed, was said to have lain wounded in a clump of bushes, picking off a dozen Indians.[92] The war ended with the retreat of the Paiutes and much victorious hooting in the region's newspapers.

In August, Ike Stockton gave a lengthy interview to a reporter from the *Denver Republican*, a newspaper that, according to the *Dolores News*, "has done more injury to Eskridge and Stockton than all other sources combined in days gone by. The spirit of justification which this paper shows now is to be commended. The correction appears much more graceful coming from the source which has done most harm."[93]

The *Denver Republican* reporter described Stockton as "a pleasant-faced, mild-mannered gentleman, who said he had a grievance…He wore a neat goatee and moustache, and had grayish-blue eyes. The face was a mild one, and rather attractive. There certainly was nothing brutal or repulsive about it."[94] The reporter went on to say that "in Durango public sympathy is entirely with Stockton. He is regarded as a quiet, peaceable and enterprising citizen."[95]

This state of affairs continued for several months, with New Mexican papers churning out stories against Stockton and Colorado papers defending him. It appeared that the Stockton gang habitually rode over the border into New Mexico, where they engaged in rustling and ruffianism and then high-tailed it back to Colorado for safety.

At the end of August, the *Dolores News* was still defending Ike Stockton against accusations that he'd been making cattle raids and robberies in New Mexico: "Ike has not been in Rio Arriba county for months and has been busy working his mines and fighting Indians all summer."[96]

However, in September, the *Dolores News* editors abruptly changed their tune. The reason was nineteen-year-old Stockton acolyte Bert Wilkinson.

Bert was "one of those town fellows who had an hello for everybody; the overgrown body covering a minute package of a brain, easily swayed, not fit for mental work but good for hours of heavy lifting, pulling, working."[97] From a prominent American family, Bert had a grandfather who was in the Indiana legislature for two decades. His father was an Indian agent and later a lawyer in Washington, D.C. Bert apparently worked part time as a janitor at the *Dolores News* and was listed as living in the same household as the editors in the 1880 census.

The event that brought about this change involved a black cowboy named Kid Thomas. He had a brother who robbed a stage near Conejos, and the brother had apparently told Kid where the loot was hidden. Thomas asked for leave from his job so he could attend his brother's trial. He knew members of the Stockton gang and told them about this loot. Dyson Eskridge and young Bert Wilkinson decided to accompany him to the brother's trial (and presumably to search for the loot), with Kid footing their travel expenses. When the trio passed through Silverton, they headed to a saloon and began drinking. Kid was reportedly the only one of the group who stayed sober. At some point, a drunken Dyson Eskridge pulled out his gun and began shooting at the lights, and Wilkinson followed suit. Silverton marshal Clate Ogsbury entered the saloon, intending to tell the boys to put their guns away. He was hit by one of the whizzing bullets and dropped dead on the spot. Bert Wilkinson and Dyson Eskridge skedaddled out the back door, leaving Kid Thomas to face the wrathful Silvertonians. Even though he hadn't been drinking or shooting, the sheriff arrested him. The next night, a lynch mob appeared at the Silverton jail, took Kid Thomas out of his cell, dragged him to a shed and lynched him.

A reward of $2,500 each was offered for Wilkinson and Eskridge. Their friend and comrade, Ike Stockton, apparently found this irresistible. He got himself appointed deputy sheriff and, along with a buddy, Durango deputy marshal Marion C. Cook, took off after the fugitives. According to Stockton's account, they found Wilkinson's trail and followed him through the wilderness for three days. Finally they came upon him sleeping in a campsite seven miles northeast of Animas City. Young Wilkinson awakened to find a gun pointing at him. They handcuffed him, and the three men rode back to Animas City. Wilkinson confessed that it was his bullet that killed the marshal. That night they kept him under heavy guard. Feelings were still high against the men who had shot the popular Ogsbury. Among the few words Wilkinson spoke was his remorse about the death of Kid Thomas: "I will tell you what I would like to say in regard to the Kid being hung up there. It was a murder when they hung him, and a foul murder too."[98]

Wilkinson was soon escorted to Silverton, fully expecting to be lynched. He was said to be in a daze, trying to figure out what he had done to cause Ike Stockton to turn against him. In Silverton, as expected, the mob soon appeared. They took Wilkinson to the same shed, where he received the same treatment as Kid Thomas.

The *Dolores News* editors were distraught over the death of their young friend, Bert Wilkinson. They were also shocked at Stockton's betrayal:

> *We knew Wilkinson when he was nothing but a great, simple, overgrown boy, generous and good of heart, and even at the time of his death his career of crime had been of very short duration. He would not have been 20 years of age until the 23^d of October next.*
>
> *While no excuse can be made for Wilkinson and his crime, we are free to say now that the man who captured him carries a blacker heart than that of Wilkinson. This may appear a queer statement coming from the one paper which has fought for him and his friends at a time when the whole country was down on them and when we lost money and friends by so doing. We staid [sic] by them through thick and thin, for friendship's sake alone. We believed them to be honest men, knowing that they were fighting against men who were notorious out-laws and cattle thieves. We have found out recently that we were on the right side of a very bad matter, and have taken pains to inquire into the life of Stockton for many years past. His record is not what it should be. Bert Wilkinson was his friend and would have fought for him at any time, of which fact Stockton was fully aware, and during the fight with the Farmington people last winter he regretted many times that Bert was not in the country to help him. They relied on one another for help, and Wilkinson had a right to expect assistance from Stockton, as he was a man of his own stripe.*[99]

The paper then presented a different version of Wilkinson's capture, as told to them by Wilkinson's sister, Mrs. Flora Pyle, who had seen her brother in jail before he was lynched. It turned out that Stockton had headed straight to Flora's home, knowing there was a good chance Wilkinson and Eskridge would show up there. Flora fed Stockton and gave him a place to sleep. The next day, as expected, Wilkinson and Eskridge arrived, hungry and cold. Eskridge was without shoes. Stockton told his friends that he was there to warn them of a lynching party on their way from Silverton. He then urged Wilkinson and Eskridge to split up. Flora gave the two men horses and provisions for several days, having extracted a promise from them to behave in future. The men all agreed to meet at a certain place, which they did. At that point, Stockton and Dyson left for half a day, after which Stockton returned without Dyson, saying they were to meet the two Eskridge brothers five miles away with fresh horses. As Bert readied his saddle, he turned to find Stockton's gun trained on him. Bert laughed, thinking it was a joke. He then stopped short when he saw the look on Stockton's face. According to Flora's account: "[Bert] said: 'Ike, do you mean it?' to which Stockton replied: 'Yes, I do mean it—money is what makes men in this country.' Bert said: 'You've got the drop on me, Ike, but I'd rather you'd killed me.' [Stockton] promised [Bert] he'd never be turned over without something to defend himself."[100]

Eskridge was also captured—by his own brother according to the *Rocky Mountain News*.[101] He was later let go, since Wilkinson confessed to the shooting.

Even though Ike Stockton had tracked down the man who killed the popular marshal, the *Dolores News* editors were not the only parties who despised him for his betrayal of Wilkinson. Less than two months later, Sheriff Watson and Deputy Sheriff Jim Sullivan, a friend of Ike's, finally moved to arrest Ike Stockton in Durango. They carried an indictment against Stockton for the murder of Aaron Barker in New Mexico the previous March.

That morning, Stockton and his comrade, M.C. Cook, rode a wagon into Durango from Animas City. Stockton got out and walked up the street while Cook stayed with the wagon. There, Cook was quietly taken into custody on other charges from New Mexico.

The sheriff intercepted Stockton and announced he was under arrest. Stockton jumped into the doorway of a building and drew his gun. Both lawmen fired. One bullet entered Stockton's thigh and another elsewhere in his leg. Stockton was supposed to be handed over to New Mexico authorities, but his leg injury was so serious that doctors had to amputate the leg at

Ike Stockton was buried in the Animas City cemetery. *Photo by Julie Pickett.*

midthigh. In the early morning hours of October 26, 1881, with his wife and two toddlers at his bedside, Ike Stockton died.

Twenty-nine-year-old Ike Stockton was buried in the Animas City cemetery. The *Durango Herald* reported that his friends "purchased a hundred dollar casket, upon the top of which was a silver-plate engraved, "Isaac T. Stockton, aged 29 years."[102]

M.C. Cook was hauled off to Texas on charges of murder, rape, arson and stock theft. In Durango, he left behind a teenage wife and a small child.

With their report of Stockton's capture and death, the *Dolores News* dryly added:

> *It is not the policy of the* News *to abuse any dead man. We gave our opinion of Stockton three weeks ago in very plain language. So soon as we*

found that we supporting [sic] *the wrong kind of a man we said so publicly and concluded to have nothing more to do with him one way or the other. He is dead; he deserved his fate—that ends it.*[103]

Postscript

In early November 1881, a man named J.K. Mills of Durango, a spiritualist, claimed he saw a vision of Ike Stockton walking down the street and being shot by the sheriff. Another man was with Stockton in the vision, Mills said, but he disappeared during the shooting. Puzzled, Mills asked around but could find no information about who this second man was. It wasn't Cook, who was under arrest back in the wagon. One day, Mills happened to see a photograph of Bert Wilkinson. In great shock, Mills announced that Bert was the man he had seen beside Stockton.

In March 1882, Port Stockton's widow, Emily Jane Cowan Stockton, married Joel Estes of the Disappointment Valley's Estes family. The elder Joel Estes was an original pioneer of Estes Park, Colorado, and is that town's namesake. Emily died in La Plata County in 1893 at the age of forty-one. She was buried in the Animas City Cemetery in an unmarked grave.

Ike's widow, Amanda Ellen Stockton, married Nathaniel Caldwell in 1882 and moved to Fresno, California. The couple had three children: Colbert, Julia and Cedric.

Chapter 6
The Tragic Tale of Mary Rose and the Cuddigans

Ten-year-old Mary Rose Matthews lost her mother as a very young girl. Her father, a Denver policeman, tried to care for her but was unable to. When he lost his job, he left his little girl in the care of neighbors and took off. In April 1883, Mary Rose was taken to St. Vincent's Orphan Asylum in Denver.

A few months later, in July 1883, she was adopted by Michael and Maggie (or Mary) Cuddigan, a ranching couple who lived about ten miles outside Ouray. Maggie's brother, John Carroll, also lived and worked on the ranch, and the Cuddigans had a baby boy, Percival. Ouray's itinerant Catholic priest, Father Robert Servant, brought the young girl to her new family.

Apparently unknown to Father Servant or the sisters at St. Vincent's, Michael Cuddigan had a reputation as a drunkard with a violent temper. Over the next months, neighbors noticed changes in Mary Rose's personality. Instead of the winsome, helpful girl that traveled from Denver, she became quiet and haggard. She was often seen with bruises. Unfortunately, nobody took action to find out what was wrong.

On a cold day in January 1884, Mary Rose's already bad luck took a turn for the worse. On January 13, a hunter found the little girl poorly clothed and unconscious lying in a haystack near the ranch house. He took her to the Cuddigans and left. When neighbors came by the house to visit, the Cuddigans told them that Mary Rose was dead. They claimed she had fallen down some stairs.

The Cuddigans quickly buried the girl in a remote corner of their property. This finally aroused suspicion in the neighbors, and they notified the coroner. W.W. Rowan, M.D., exhumed the small body and did a post mortem. Rowan's testimony at the subsequent inquest horrified the community:

> *I reside in Ouray. Am 34 years of age and a surgeon and physician by occupation. Have made a post mortem examination on the body of a dead girl about ten or eleven years of age, name unknown: unclothed the body and found both feet frozen, peeling off of the outer skin of both legs and both thighs, showing strong indications of having been frozen: the skin on lower half of right leg peeled off and on the right knee four wounds with the skin peeled off from frost: on the left knee was a cut of two inches over knee cap and three wounds on left thigh with partial dislocation of the skin: on the left hand fingers have been frozen; several wounds on forearm, bruised elbow and considerable discoloration of arm: on the right hand her four fingers and thumb had been frozen completely to the second joint with numbers of wounds on the right arm; on the forehead a little to the left of center, found she had received a severe blow by some blunt instrument: also on the rear portion of head found a very large wound, about the size of a silver dollar, caused by some blunt instrument.*
>
> *I opened the skull and found the posterior portion of the brain considerably engorged with a very large clot of blood weighing fifteen grains, which, to the best of my knowledge and belief, and from the impoverished condition of the body from treatment received, did cause the death of the deceased.*[104]

Several neighbors, although obviously too late to help the little girl, testified on Mary Rose's behalf at the inquest. A man named C.R. Brandenberry said:

> *About eight or ten days ago I went to Cuddigan's ranch for the purpose of hunting stray cattle. Saw this child on the hay stack: she crawled by [unreadable] her hands were [unreadable] up and she did not seem to notice anything: her face was bruised, also the back of her head: D.S. Duffield was with me: we thought she looked strange and spoke of it afterwards. It was a very cold day.*[105]

Another neighbor, L. B. Montgomery, testified: "I own a ranch about a mile and a quarter west of Cuddigan's: went to his place about one month ago on business: saw the girl washing dishes: noticed she was acting strangely: Spoke of it afterwards: saw her face bruised; am nearly certain she was barefooted: she seemed to be very dull of comprehension."[106]

The coroner's jury ruled that Michael Cuddigan, Maggie Cuddigan and Maggie's brother, John Carroll, had killed Mary Rose. Sheriff Rawles arrested the trio and held them under heavy guard at the Delmonico Hotel, which stood at that time on Main Street in Ouray between Fourth and Fifth Avenues. At the time, Mrs. Cuddigan was many months pregnant and "would soon have become a mother."[107]

During the investigation into Mary Rose's death, the coroner opened the doors and allowed the public in to view the child's battered and frost-bitten body. Not surprisingly—and perhaps for some out of a sense of guilt at their own inaction—feelings among the townsfolk ran high against the prisoners. In his usual style, David Day of the *Solid Muldoon* wrote scathing editorials against the prisoners. He was later accused of suggesting "that lynching was the proper thing to do."[108]

Several days later, on January 18, just past midnight, a mob of masked men powered their way past guards at the Delmonico and took all three prisoners. A reporter described what happened next:

> *Guards had been posted* [by the mob] *at various points along the streets, and all who came out into the street were ordered to return, which they did. Mike Cuddigan and Mary* [Maggie?] *Cuddigan were hurried down Third street, pleading and begging piteously for mercy until Tommy Andrews' cabin was reached, where the avengers halted. The rope was placed around Cuddigan's neck and he was swung up to the ridge pole of the cabin, while a small tree just across the road was converted into a gallows for Mary Cuddigan.*[109]

After lynching Michael Cuddigan, the mob took the pregnant Mrs. Cuddigan to the tree across the road and lynched her. This was the first time a woman was lynched in Colorado.

The fate of John Carroll was a bit less harsh:

After Cuddigan and his wife were strung up, John Carroll, a brother of Mrs. Cuddigan, and who had been charged with being one of the murderers of little Mary Rose Matthews, was taken in a buggy and driven several miles out of town. They then stopped and were soon joined by several others of masked vigilantes who rode on horseback. That the mob was cool and conservative and intelligent is shown in Carroll's case. They had hung Cuddigan and his wife because they considered there was no doubt of their guilt. There was some question of Carroll's guilt. However, they had taken Carroll to a more secluded spot where they would more fully investigate his complicity. Carroll pleaded piteously for his life. He said he was not at the Cuddigan ranch on the night of the murder, had not been there for several days, and could not therefore be held in any way responsible for the crime. He said he knew about the murder, but made himself an accessory after the act by keeping it quiet, simply for the protection of his sister.[110]

Despite his pleas, the vigilantes strung him up. However, they had a change of heart and lowered him to the ground. Apparently deciding that the law no longer wanted him, they set him free on his word that he would never return to the area.

After the lynching, the mob put their handiwork on display in Ouray. The *Leadville Herald* reported, "The bodies of Cuddigan and wife were lying side by side today and were visited by hundreds of people. Their features are terribly distorted, even showing that they had died a horrible death from strangulation."[111] Also on display was Mary Rose's miserable bed, "consist[ing] of four gunny sacks basted together, nothing more. Both sides of the gunny sacks were blood stained."[112]

Newspapers reported that the Cedar Hill Cemetery refused to take the bodies. Michael Cuddigan's brothers also refused to have anything to do with it. Finally, the coroner had the Cuddigans buried on their ranch.

A few locals spoke up in defense of the Cuddigans, saying that they were a well-known and respectable ranching couple. The Catholic priest, Father Servant, who had given Mary Rose to the Cuddigans, reportedly refused to officiate at the couple's funeral. However, the man described as a "little French priest"[113] spoke up sharply against the lynch mob. Folks in Ouray

Wicked Tales from Ouray, San Juan and La Plata Counties

Ouray in 1901. *Courtesy Library of Congress.*

didn't care for the rebuke, so they circulated a petition inviting him to leave. He refused.

Some folks were horrified at the lynching of a woman—particularly a woman in an advanced state of pregnancy. However, most were so disgusted by what had been done to Mary Rose that they openly approved of the lynching. This latter group included a physician who examined Mary Rose's body. Dr. B.S. Tedmon wrote a shocking letter to the *Fort Collins Courier*:

> *While I believe in law and justice as the proper method to determine the amount of punishment to be inflicted for most crimes, I must surely claim, after a personal examination of the victim this morning…I can now see how the people of Ouray were justified in hanging the Cuddigan fiends. And I believe could you have stood with me and seen the lacerated, bruised, cut and frozen form of the once beautiful and innocent child, you would say that hanging was too easy, too mild a punishment for such wretches.*[114]

Tedmon went on to describe Mary Rose's injuries in horrifying detail, concluding the description with, "Add to this the fact as given by several physicians upon examination that the child had been outraged by Cuddigan himself."[115]

The *Denver News* echoed other statements made by Dr. Tedmon, that the act of a lynch mob was in direct response to the fact that the justice system in Colorado wasn't sufficiently strict:

> *The cure, in a large measure rests with our courts and juries. They have been too lax in the judgment of men who have committed murder. Not one conviction for murder in the first degree has been recorded in this State for fifty cold-blooded murders committed. A feeble prosecution, a strong defense, and an easy-going jury can always be relied upon to save a murderer from the gallows under the present system of administering the criminal code in Colorado.*
>
> *Mob violence is dangerous and disgraceful to the State, but it is encouraged, and to the unthinking, it is in some measure justified, by the failure of justice in our courts.*[116]

Mary Rose was briefly reburied in Ouray but was once more dug up and carted off to Denver, where her decaying remains were once again put on display for the gawkers of Denver to see. Finally, little Mary Rose was put to rest in Denver.

No one was ever arrested for the lynchings.

Postscript

Percival Cuddigan was raised by Michael Cuddigan's brother, Henry. Michael and Maggie Cuddigan's estate was put in trust for the boy. The 1900 and 1910 census records show him living in Ridgeway with his cousin Charley Kelley.

In 1902, the St. Vincent's Orphan Asylum in Denver burned down. All two hundred children in residence were rescued.

Over the years, a number of area residents have reported the sight of a beaten waif of a girl, usually alongside a road or near a barn. But when they tried to reach out to her, she always disappeared.

Chapter 7

The Famous and Infamous Days of the San Juans

David Frakes Day was one of the most famous—and notorious—newsmen in Colorado's frontier days. His caustic wit and love for a good fight earned him plenty of admirers and enemies.

Born in Ohio in 1847, he enlisted in the Union army at fifteen. He fought at the famous and bloody battles of Shiloh and Vicksburg under General Ulysses S. Grant. He was also captured several times and escaped from the notorious Andersonville and other prisons. In a rare achievement, young Day was decorated with a Medal of Honor for his Civil War service. In later years, he became an honorary colonel in the Colorado National Guard.

After the war, Day had trouble finding his feet, and he drifted around for a time until he found himself in Missouri. There he became a storekeeper, married and started a family. At the age of thirty, facing bankruptcy, he headed on his own to Colorado, planning to send for his family when he was settled. There he apparently presented himself as a newspaper editor, though his experience was limited to writing anonymous articles for a Missouri paper.[117]

With a little financial help from new frontier friends, he started what would become his famous (or infamous) Ouray newspaper, the *Solid Muldoon*. From this "pulpit," he began his raucous, long-running editorial on the doings of western Colorado.

His courage and bigger-than-life personality served him well for the rough and dangerous world of the San Juans. Day was among rescuers when, in

A young David Day distinguished himself fighting under General Ulysses S. Grant at Vicksburg *(shown)* and Shiloh. *Courtesy Library of Congress.*

December 1883, a huge snowslide swept over the boardinghouse at the Virginius mine, located in the towering Sneffels range. Though four miners were smothered, Day helped pull five others still alive out of the boardinghouse.[118]

Despite his reputation as a tough guy and a good citizen, Day's stinging editorials earned him many enemies. He delighted in lampooning other public figures, and most were not amused. One of these was Attorney Theron Stevens, a courageous man who later became a judge and denounced the military takeover of Telluride during that town's labor troubles. According to one story, Stevens finally had enough of Day's attacks. Early one morning he accosted the editor in the street, challenging him to a duel. The men walked over to the Muldoon office where Day picked up a .45. As the two headed for the town limits, Day suddenly suggested that they needed a witness. Stevens agreed, and Day ran off to find someone. He returned with the sheriff, who, as expected, put an end to the plan.[119]

Day routinely went after railroad men and big mining interests. He published a blacklist of corporations he didn't like. He supported mining but complained about how the beautiful countryside was being plundered by "Silver Kings" from the east. He raged at the Denver and Rio Grande for not putting a spur into Ouray. When the railroad finally built the line, Day fought a new war against them over exorbitant freight rates. Day also waged endless battles with other members of the press, accusing them of being boosters for big corporate interests.

Some of Day's newspaper campaigns were highly questionable, such as his fuming editorials during the Mary Rose Matthews case, which were blamed by some for inciting the lynch mob that killed the Cuddigans.

In 1892, Day moved to Durango. He soon retired the *Solid Muldoon* after merging with the *Herald*, calling the new paper the *Durango Democrat*. With that, he announced his intention of being the Democratic voice among a cluster of Republican newspapers. By this time, he was famous throughout the state and was often quoted in other newspapers.

Day professed at times to be a friend of labor but complained often and loudly about labor union "agitators." In November 1902, when his own union printers went on strike, he locked them out and hired nonunion men. Unions and others issued a boycott against the *Durango Democrat*, and many merchants withdrew their ads. Members of the union started a new paper, called the *Trade's Journal*. Most of the writing was done by Frank Hartman—probably the same Hartman who expended so much effort defending Ike Stockton twenty years earlier. Hartman and Day then made a full-time job out of roasting each other in their columns.[120]

In May 1903, the war of words escalated into a "shooting scrape" on Main Street in Durango. That evening Frank Hartman was talking to a man named Dan Muser in front of the Elnora saloon. David Day approached the men and asked Muser if he were associated with the *Trade's Journal*, saying anyone who was "is a s—— of a b——."[121] Suddenly, guns were drawn, and a gun battle ensued. Though thirteen shots were exchanged from about eight feet apart, the only injury was a slight wound in Hartman's thigh. It wasn't clear who fired first.

Day also engaged in a war of words with John G. Higgins of the *Durango Telegraph*. Upon a challenge from Higgins, Day wrote that Higgins was "as dirty a liar, as dirty a scoundrel, as dirty an ingrate, as dirty a tool and as base and complete a degenerate as ever lived, we accept his challenge to have it out on the streets the first time we meet. God never created as dirty a dog, without that dog was regularly whelped, as John G. Higgins."[122]

As he generally managed to do, Day somehow escaped having to "have it out on the streets" with his "dirty" foe.

Day's personal life appeared to have its own troubles. He and his wife, Victoria Folck Day, had eight children, but three of them died as babies or toddlers. The 1900 census shows him apparently living with his son, Stanley, and family, though Victoria was still alive at the time.

In July 1903, after a quarter century, David Day announced his farewell from the newspaper business, though it was only a partial retirement. His son-in-law, Thomas Tully, took over the reins at the *Durango Democrat*. David Frakes Day died June 22, 1914, in Durango. He was buried at Riverside Cemetery in Denver.

David's death was not the end of the Day saga, however. His son, Roderick Day, continued his father's tradition of making war with other newspaper editors.

David Day was buried at Denver's Riverside Cemetery. *Photo by the author.*

Wicked Tales from Ouray, San Juan and La Plata Counties

Born in Saline, Missouri, in 1874, Rod Day married Mabel Clapp in January 1905 in San Miguel County. The couple had three daughters and a son. Somewhere along the line, he took over management of the *Durango Democrat*. On Monday, April 24, 1922, in a scene reminiscent of the elder Day, an ongoing dispute between Rod Day and William Lyon Wood, editor of the *Durango Evening Herald*, degenerated into deadly gunfire.

Like Rod Day, William Wood had a locally famous father—he was the son of Dave Wood, the celebrated pioneer and freighter who built the roads between Montrose and the San Juan region. Dave Wood is credited with creating the lively trade that developed between the mining region and the farming communities to the north.

The younger Wood had previously worked for Rod Day at the *Durango Democrat*. It's not clear whether their private animosity began during that time or later when William Wood became editor of the *Evening Herald*. Their very public war started in early April 1922, when the *Montrose Press* published a short article criticizing Rod Day for his opposition to the Volstead Act, which brought Prohibition to the nation. William Wood reprinted the article in the *Evening Herald*. This prompted a rebuttal on Day's part in the next morning's paper, followed by another snipe from Wood that evening. This process continued for some days, the attacks and counterattacks finally degenerating into a highly personal public squabble. Day accused employees of the *Herald* of breaking the law. Wood mentioned "drunken sprees said to have been indulged in by Day about a year ago, and which finally are said to have resulted in Day winding up in a hospital, following which it is said he was forced to take a several months' vacation from his work."[123] Day countered with stories about Wood's "'bitter past,' which he said needed 'fumigation' and continued by making some remarks about Wood's divorce and other escapades in Durango."[124]

Finally, at ten o'clock on a Monday morning, in front of a pool hall on Main Street in Durango, the two men met and began arguing. In view of several witnesses, Rod Day pulled a gun and shot William Wood twice. Wood fell to the ground. Bystanders rushed him to Durango's Mercy Hospital. There, three hours later, the twenty-nine-year-old veteran of World War I died of a gunshot wound to the neck.

Accompanied by the owner of the *Durango Herald*, J.H. McDevitt Jr., and many friends, colleagues and members of the American Legion, Wood's body was escorted through the streets of Durango. The tolling of the city bell marked the procession. They arrived at the train station and put his body on board for transport to Montrose. Wood's widow, his second wife, Lillian, was reported to be so overcome that she was confined to her bed and could not attend the funeral. The couple had only been married for about nine months, and she was pregnant. William Wood was buried in the Wood family plot in Montrose's Cedar Cemetery. After the service, Wood's mother traveled to Durango to help her daughter-in-law.

Meanwhile, Rod Day was arrested and held without bail. The inquest was held Wednesday, during which twenty-five people testified. Witnesses on the street that morning reported that Wood had been looking for Day. "Wood was then asked by these witnesses if he were armed. Wood replied, 'No! All I need I've got in my good right arm.'"[125] Witnesses also said that Day first struck Wood with a carpenter's square, and Wood punched him in the face, then "backed into the gutter and was from 8 to 20 feet from Day and turned in a sideways position when Day opened fire."[126] The fatal bullet hit Wood in the back of the neck, traveling upward into his brain.

The coroner's jury ruled that Wood died of a gunshot wound at the hands of Rod Day. The famed local firm of Russell & Reese agreed to defend Day. He was charged with first-degree murder, to which he had entered a plea of self-defense. On May 9, after Day had spent two weeks in jail, he was released on $10,000 bond.

His trial took place eight months after the shooting, in December 1922. At that time, Lillian Wood, the widow, was still under the constant care of her physician. Her baby had been born but she was still so distraught about her husband's death that both she and the baby had "been despaired of at various times since the baby's birth."[127]

The jury consisted of eleven farmers and a forest ranger. A parade of witnesses testified for the prosecution that Day shot Woods "while the latter had his back turned."[128]

Rod Day took the stand in his own defense, testifying that Wood was angry with him for bringing Wood's previous divorce into the newspaper fight. He said Wood struck him in the face, stunning him with the blow. He then said he drew his revolver and shot Wood as the latter came at him again.[129]

Roderick Day's grave in the Day family plot. *Courtesy Greenmount Cemetery, Durango.*

After a weeklong trial, the jury went out and deliberated for thirty hours. They went through thirteen ballots before finally returning with a verdict. Rod Day was pronounced not guilty and was free to go.

Rod Day died in 1940 and was buried at Durango's Greenmount Cemetery.

Chapter 8

A Colorado Range War

The Cox-Truby Feud

One recurring theme of the Old West was the animosity between cattlemen and sheepmen. Their range wars brought violence and death to many pioneers. Cattlemen considered themselves superior, perhaps because they were usually mounted on horses, while sheepmen were often on foot. Some cattlemen insisted that sheep munched the wild grasses too close to the root and drove other livestock away, allegedly leaving behind miles of barren wasteland. Most likely the essential problem lay in the simple fact that sheepmen competed with cattlemen for grazing rights to public lands.

In the early twentieth century, the San Juan region played host to its own range war. Known as the Cox-Truby feud, it came to a bloody climax in 1911. However, the trouble between Ike Cox and the Truby family had been simmering for years.

Both families came to the Colorado–New Mexico border region from Texas. The large Cox family arrived in the region in the late 1870s with several thousand head of cattle. They settled just south of the border in New Mexico, along the Animas River in a place called Cox's Crossing. Later the name was changed to Cedar Hill. The Trubys arrived in 1899, settling on a chunk of the "Ute Strip," part of the Ute Reservation that the government opened up to homesteaders. The family was headed by Robert Truby and the matriarch, Elizabeth. They settled near today's Bondad, in La Plata County with their five sons: John, Henry, William, David and Sam. The family also included a three-year-old granddaughter, Ida Hale, daughter of eighteen-year-old Sarah Truby Hale, who had died in 1899 in Rico, Colorado.

In February 1904, the *Durango Democrat* reported that one of the Truby sons, Dave, was brought in on charges of cattle stealing. He was released on $500 bail.[130] A year later, the *Telluride Daily Journal* reported that another Truby son, William, had been arrested on similar charges:

> *Saturday afternoon Wm. Truby, a ranchman, was arrested, brought to town and held under $500 bond on a charge of stealing cattle. Truby had been selling dressed beef in town without exhibiting the hides and brands. The sheriff went out to his ranch and was unable to find any hides, when an information was sworn out. It is said neighbors have been missing cattle from their herds.*[131]

By law, people selling beef in town were required to prove their ownership of the beef by displaying the hide and brand. The charges against William "Bill" Truby had been brought by another cattleman, a Mr. Coppinger, who presumably believed Truby had stolen the cattle from him.[132]

At the end of March 1905, Bill Truby went to trial; the case resulted in a hung jury. The following August, his case was back on the docket, with another charge of larceny tacked on. He was defended by famed Durango attorney Charles A. Johnson. Newspapers did not report the result of these charges.

Years later, in January 1911, arrests on charges of cattle theft were again reported against "two men named Carter and Truby,"[133] which could refer to one of the Truby brothers and their neighbor, Charley Carter, who had a close relationship with the Trubys. On January 12, 1911, twenty-seven-year-old William Truby married fourteen-year-old Cordula Carter, the daughter of Charley Carter.

For several years, the Cox and Truby clans both ran cattle in the Cox Canyon region in Colorado, west of the Animas River. The trouble between Ike Cox and the Trubys started when Ike Cox decided to run sheep in the area. The Trubys were shocked and angered by this turn of events. In 1905, Bill Truby reportedly rampaged through the Cox sheep herd, trampling sheep and beating Ike Cox over the head with a bridle rein, telling him to get out of the area.[134]

This was only the opening salvo in what became years of threats and counterthreats. Tensions eased in 1909 when Ike moved his sheep north of Bayfield to the Pine River area. There he grazed them peacefully for a couple years. However, early in 1911, he moved the herd back to their original grazing lands and trouble instantly started. On April 16, 1911, two of the Truby sons, Sam and Bill, met Ike Cox and another man named Calvin Barrows on the banks of the Florida River, where they fought it out without the use of weapons. Unfortunately, the fistfight did not settle the problem.

What happened next wasn't witnessed by anyone, so the story is a case of "he said–he said." What is clear is that on April 23, 1911, somewhere on a mesa overlooking the Florida River, Bill and Sam Truby met Ike Cox and exchanged insults. All three were on horseback.

In Ike Cox's version of the story, he wanted to avoid more trouble, so he rode away. When the brothers chased him and tried to pull him off his horse, he drew his weapon and fired.

Sam Truby's story differed considerably. He claimed that Cox had purchased ammunition that morning and gone looking for them. When Cox spotted them, he called Bill a foul name and shot him. Cox then tried to shoot Sam but hit his horse instead.

What is known for certain is that gunfire erupted and the twenty-eight-year-old newlywed, Bill Truby, fell from his horse, dead from a gunshot wound. Sam Truby, whose horse was shot, chased Ike Cox on foot, shooting after him with a rifle. None of these shots hit home.

Ike Cox rode into Durango and turned himself in. The coroner's jury ruled that William Truby had been killed by Ike Cox, and Cox was charged with premeditated murder. The post mortem revealed that William Truby had been shot in the chest.

Cox hired the celebrated firm of Reese & Russell to defend him. After about ten days in jail, he bonded out for $10,000 on May 3.

Bill Truby's family buried him in Greenmount Cemetery. Bill had left behind his beautiful fourteen-year-old wife, Cordula (née Carter), whom he had just married three months earlier. He also left behind a very angry Truby family.

Meanwhile, Cox had apparently had enough of the war. He sold his sheep herd and his land and moved with his wife and five children to Pagosa Springs.

William Truby's grave at the Truby family plot. *Courtesy Greenmount Cemetery, Durango.*

Truby family marker at Greenmount Cemetery, Durango. *Photo by Lindsay Eppich.*

About a month after the shooting, Ike Cox was staying in Durango consulting with Ben Russell, his attorney, about his upcoming murder trial. According to the *Durango Wage Earner*, "The Trubys had made threats that [Cox] would never live to meet his trial…his friends and bondsmen had insisted that he remain in the city, in the supposed safety of the officials' care. He has been sleeping in the court house and has been carefully avoiding any meeting with the Truby boys or members of that clique."[135]

One night at about ten o'clock, Cox and Deputy Sheriff William F. Sease went for a walk. As they ambled up Tenth Street, between Main and Second Avenues, they heard footsteps on the wooden sidewalk behind them. A man came up on their left, and they exchanged greetings. Suddenly, the man produced a .38 and fired three shots at Ike Cox. The first bullet hit Cox in the small of the back and came out near his abdomen. The second blasted into his jaw near the neck. The third shot went wild.[136]

The shooter escaped, running in the direction of the railroad yards.

Cox was rushed to the private Ochsner Hospital at 805 East Fifth Avenue.[137] Though he was still alive, most newspapers reported that he'd been assassinated and referred to him as the "murdered man." It was unanimously declared that his chances of surviving his injuries were not good.

Defending himself against grumblings among the citizenry and press, Deputy Sease said he'd been unable to fire any shots at the gunman—first, because Cox had fallen into his arms; and second, because there were too many people around.

Rumors quickly circulated that the shooter was Bill Truby's adolescent widow, Cordula Truby, dressed up in men's clothing. She had reportedly come into town the night before on the "Red Apple" train and was seen in town that day. Another Truby in town during the shooting was Sam. He had been enjoying a treat in an ice cream parlor while the shooting took place. Newspapers reported that two Durango policemen were with Truby at the time, giving rise to speculation that he'd been keeping the officers busy while the crime was being committed.

Public sentiment, which already tended to favor Ike Cox, now grew loud in support of the injured man. He and his family had been living in the region for decades and had a good reputation and numerous friends. The *Bayfield Blade* reported that his bond had been supplied by "the most influential citizens of Durango."[138] The Trubys, on the other hand, still had cases pending on charges of stealing cattle. One newspaper in particular, the *Durango Herald*, went out of its way to lambaste the Trubys and print favorable stories about Cox. Sam Truby later sued that newspaper for libel, causing the editor, named Munson, to be arrested, all of which created a further flap in the regional papers.

Shortly after the shooting of Ike Cox, two men were arrested and interrogated by authorities. They were apparently associated with the Trubys and were thought to know something about a plot to kill Cox. However, this led nowhere, and the men were released. Sam Truby was also arrested and held on $4,000 bond, which his mother and friends of the family soon paid. Cordula Truby was not arrested and was allowed to leave town. A $750 reward was offered for the shooter.

Meanwhile, Ike Cox was still hanging on in critical condition in the hospital. His family traveled from Pagosa Springs to be near him. Within a week, reports of his condition were much more optimistic, and Dr. Benjamin Ochsner, celebrated as the best doctor in the four corners region, announced that Cox would probably recover.

A week or two after the shooting, authorities arrested a young fellow named Andrew "Shorty" Ruple, a goatherd described as "rather light in the upper

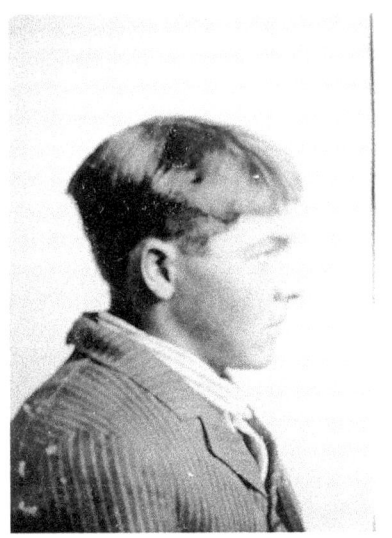

Young Andrew Ruple may have been smitten by Bill Truby's widow, fourteen-year-old Cordula. *Colorado State Archives.*

story."[139] He worked for Charley Carter, father of Cordula Truby. Deputy Sease had apparently recognized him, and authorities had been hunting him down. Sheriff Tim McCluer and another man named Lines located Ruple at a goat camp on the Florida River near Bondad and brought him in. Sources differ on Ruple's age, but based on census and reformatory records, he was somewhere between fifteen and seventeen at the time of the shooting.

Ruple quickly confessed, claiming that he had been paid to assassinate Cox. In his statement, he said that Cordula Truby had first approached him shortly after Bill's death a month earlier. Later, Sam and Dave Truby and Charley Carter also worked on him. He also implicated the family matriarch, Elizabeth Truby. (The father, Robert, had died in 1904.) Although Ruple initially resisted their request, he said, "I finally agreed and Carter promised me 'Mancos Pearl' [a horse] and all of his goats and Dave promised 500 head of sheep and three good horses."[140] The celebrated Mancos Pearl, ridden by Sam Truby, had recently won a horse race.

Sam Truby and Charley Carter were both arrested (rearrested, in Sam's case). Remaining members of the Truby clan made themselves scarce. A couple months later, New Mexico authorities searching for the Trubys reported being fired on from ambush, blaming the attack on Sam, Dave and Henry Truby, along with a fourth man.[141] No one was hurt in the encounter, and the men escaped, leaving behind a wagon and some horses.

Within a few weeks, Ruple was tried and convicted on two counts of assault with intent to kill and one of conspiracy. His sentence was three to thirty-four years. Because of his youth, he was sent to the reformatory at Buena Vista, where he arrived June 25, 1911. There he rapidly gained points for his good behavior. On May 29, 1912, after serving only eleven months, he was released on parole.

Meanwhile, Ike Cox recovered from his injuries. In late November 1911, he stood trial for the murder of Bill Truby. The star witnesses were Ike Cox and Sam Truby, each of whom told their different versions of what happened. Cox's story about being chased on horseback by the Truby brothers had been corroborated by the pattern of horse tracks found at the scene.[142] After a trial of nearly two weeks, the jury went out for half an hour. They returned with a verdict of not guilty.

Six months later, in June 1912, another trial was held, this time removed to Silverton. Sam and Dave Truby, Cordula Truby, Elizabeth Truby and

Charley Carter faced charges of conspiracy to kill Ike Cox. They were defended en masse by attorneys Charles Johnson and James Pulliam. Assisting Prosecutor George W. Lane were Ike Cox's attorneys, Ben Russell and Willis Reese of Durango. The prosecution's star witness was Andrew Ruple, who had just been released on parole. Andrew got on the stand and testified about how the defendants had hired him to kill Cox.

Defense Attorney Johnson presented an array of witnesses who testified that Andrew Ruple was a liar and a "tough character." Cordula, who had since remarried to George Henry of Aztec, New Mexico, testified that Ruple had told her, "I am going to do something for you. I am going to kill Ike Cox."[143] Another Truby brother, Henry, testified that Ruple had considered Bill Truby his best friend and did the shooting out of revenge.

After retiring for twenty-three minutes to deliberate, the jury returned with the same verdict for each of the defendants: not guilty.

Feelings around this trial ran high, and friends of Cox were enraged at the verdict. As a testament to this, Defense Attorney Charles Johnson, on his return to Durango from Silverton on the train, was assaulted by a Cox ally, Robin Frazier of Elco, who'd been a witness for the prosecution.[144]

Things did not work out well for the Cox family in Pagosa Springs. That July, Cox was injured in a serious riding accident. In October 1912, only a few months after the latest acquittals, the Cox family returned to the Cedar Hill area. Not surprisingly, the feud was instantly taken up again. Within a few weeks, shots were exchanged between the parties, though no one was hurt.

However, the war took another deadly turn that November. Again, there were two different versions of the story—the Truby version and the Cox version.

What is known is that in mid-November, Sam Truby and a companion were in Cox Canyon, southwest of Bondad. Also present in the canyon were Ike Cox and two companions. The two sides spotted each other. Scrambling around among the scrub and rocks, the warring parties engaged in a gun battle, at the end of which Sam Truby lay in the dirt, seriously wounded. The bullet had entered the top of Truby's right shoulder, passed through the lungs and came out under the shoulder blade. His lone companion, David McCullom, was also injured in the leg. McCullom stayed with Truby for a good hour, cradling his head. Finally, Truby's horse wandered near enough for McCullom to catch hold of it, and he rode off to the Truby ranch for help. Members of the clan rushed to Cox Canyon to sit with Sam,

Samuel Truby only lived about a year and a half longer than his brother, Bill. *Courtesy Greenmount Cemetery, Durango.*

while others ran for Dr. Howard Lingenfelter, who managed to drive an automobile to the site and pick up Sam. They took him to Mercy Hospital in Durango, where, early the next morning, Sam Truby died.

Ike Cox and his companions—his nephew John Graves, and Jesse Carmen (or Harmon)—turned themselves in to Sheriff McCluer in Durango. The three men faced arraignment on November 10, at which time they pleaded not guilty. They bonded out at $10,000 each.

On November 14, 1912, Sam Truby was buried near his brother, William, in the Truby family plot at Durango's Greenmount Cemetery.

The following March, Cox and his friends stood trial for the murder of Sam Truby. The trial lasted ten days, and numerous witnesses testified about the longstanding feud. At one point, while listening to the physical details of Sam Truby's injury, one of the jurors fainted.

The defense was able to show that Ike Cox's life had been under constant threat from the Trubys ever since the death of Bill Truby. They also insisted that Truby had spotted Cox and his companions in the canyon and was lying in wait for them. After Truby and McCullom attacked, the others managed to hide among the rocks and stage a counterattack.

David McCullom's story was the opposite. He testified that he and Sam were riding the range looking for cattle. They spotted Ike and his friends and decided to head home to avoid trouble. While riding back through Cox Canyon, they were ambushed from above.

The jury went out at 9:20 p.m. on Saturday. After two hours and twenty minutes, they returned with a verdict of not guilty.

Immediately after the verdict was announced, all three men were arrested again, charged with the attempted murder of Dave McCullom. They were soon released on $1,000 bond each. Before the month was out, these charges were dismissed.

Postscript

After the trial, Ike Cox announced that he was moving to Arizona, but the change was apparently short lived. In September 1914, he ran for sheriff in La Plata County on the Republican ticket. In 1920, Cox struck out for Peru, where he had apparently purchased some land. He left his wife and family to wait for him, saying he would send for them. He wrote to friends in the Durango and Ignacio area, talking about the weather in Peru and cheap prices and the quality of the cattle.[145] The venture didn't last however, as he returned in December 1921. He reported that the land didn't turn out to fit the description, and there was a "revolution in progress, the party, which had dwindled to ten, finding themselves between the opposing armies."[146] The promoter of the Peruvian scheme, a Mr. Schoenfelt, was soon under investigation by U.S. officials. Subsequently, Ike Cox made several appearances in the region, giving lectures about his South American adventures.

The surviving Truby brothers—Henry, Dave and John—continued to live in the region, and some of their descendants are still there.

By all accounts, Ike Cox's would-be assassin, Andrew Ruple, managed to stay out of trouble after serving his eleven months at Buena Vista. He later married and had children.

Chapter 9
"The Utes Must Go"

The ancestors of modern-day Utes have lived in the Colorado region for centuries, probably over a thousand years. Around the time of Columbus, Ute territory ranged across Colorado, Utah, Arizona, New Mexico, Texas, Oklahoma, Kansas and Wyoming. The Ute Nation consists of half a dozen or so related tribes, including the Uncompaghre, or Tabeguache, and White River (today's Northern Utes); the Weeminuches (Mountain Utes); and the Mouaches and Capotes (Southern Utes). Early Spanish expeditions into the territory first mentioned the Utes in the early 1600s. The 1700s brought occasional Spanish trade missions and skirmishes between the Utes and Spaniards, who controlled New Mexico. Still, the Utes were left largely undisturbed until the arrival of large numbers of Anglos in the late 1800s.

After some initial hostility in the 1850s, the Utes generally tried to maintain friendly relations with Anglos and the U.S. government. One great advocate for the Utes during this period was Christopher "Kit" Carson. Though Carson used a brutal "scorched earth" policy to remove the Navajo to the desolate Bosque Redondo reservation in eastern New Mexico, he maintained a lifelong friendship with the Utes.

In 1868, a new treaty created a Ute reservation covering most of the western third of Colorado, with the charismatic Ouray as principal chief. The Ute Nation did not particularly designate a single chief of all the Ute

Wicked Tales from Ouray, San Juan and La Plata Counties

Right: Though he was ruthless with the Navajo, Kit Carson was a lifelong friend of the Utes. *Courtesy Library of Congress.*

Below: Chief Ouray and his second wife, Chipeta, worked tirelessly to keep the Utes in Colorado. *Courtesy Library of Congress.*

tribes, but Ouray's language and diplomatic skills and willingness to talk eventually made him the "go-to" man for U.S. officials. He and his second wife, Chipeta, became famous among both Anglos and Utes.

Born in Taos, New Mexico, in 1833, Ouray was Uncompaghre Ute on his mother's side and Jicarilla Apache on his father's side. As an adult, he spoke Ute, Apache, Spanish and English. By all standards, he possessed a superior intellect and keen understanding of what lay ahead for the Ute Nation. After the Pikes Peak gold rush in the late 1850s, Ouray visited Denver City and saw for himself the tens of thousands of Anglos pouring into the region. At a time when most Ute leaders did not want to negotiate with the United States, he was able to convince them that they had no other option but to strive for a binding treaty with the invaders. The 1868 treaty he negotiated was "considered to be one of the most favorable ever won from the United States government by an Indian tribe."[147] The treaty established two agencies for the Utes: the White River Agency and the Rio de Los Piños (Pine River).

In the 1870s, white activity in western Colorado geared up with the discovery of gold and silver in the San Juans. A second treaty in 1873, the Brunot Agreement, deleted a hefty slice of the original reservation. During these negotiations, a wary Ouray became convinced that the U.S. government could not control the white settlers rushing into the San Juan region. After a week of haggling, the Utes finally agreed to allow mining operations in the San Juans, but they retained their hunting rights to the area. A new Ute agency was established at Ignacio, Colorado.

The boundaries of the Brunot Treaty were never properly publicized and it was fraught with problems. White settlers moved into areas that still belonged to the Utes. The new Ute agent, Major W.D. Wheeler, promised to keep the whites out and said he'd report it to higher ups. The issue was handed to members of Congress who promptly forgot about it. Congress finally took action in 1878, by which time whites had settled on the land. The federal government asked them to move, and the settlers demanded repayment for their improvements. Instead of paying off the white settlers, the government chose to pay $10,000 to the Utes to surrender the land.

Not all Utes agreed with Chief Ouray's policy of détente and negotiation. His Ute enemies tried several times to kill him, including even Chipeta's brother, Sapawanero (or Sapinero). According to Sidney Jocknick, an early Ute agency employee, this particular plot was conceived by five subchiefs, with Sapawanero chosen to do the deed. Sapawanero hid himself at a blacksmith's and waited for Ouray to arrive with his horse. The blacksmith somehow warned Ouray. When Sapawanero attacked Ouray with an ax, the latter was ready. The two men battled it out hand to hand, and Ouray was the victor. He stopped short of killing him, however, out of consideration for Chipeta. According to Jocknick, "Had it not been for Chipeta, Ouray would have shown him no mercy, for he was incensed to indignation at Sapinero's treachery."[148] Interestingly, Sapawanero soon resumed his former position as one of Ouray's most trusted advisors.

As more Anglos moved into the region, the limitations placed on them by the presence of the reservation began chafing. Cries came up that "the Utes must go." Newspapermen such as William B. Vickers of the *Denver Tribune* published incendiary articles about the "Ute menace," indiscriminately blaming the Utes for various murders, thefts, forest fires and other crimes. Frederick Pitkin, Colorado's governor from 1879 to 1883, ran on an anti-Ute platform.

The situation came to a boiling point in September 1879 with the Meeker Massacre. In 1878, Nathaniel Meeker had been named agent of the White River Ute agency. He had been founder of the Union Colony, a farming cooperative in Greeley, Colorado, in 1870. Unlike earlier, more successful Ute agents, Meeker was a sanctimonious, narrow-minded man. He had no experience with American Indians and didn't bother to learn anything about them. Instead he tried to get them to call him "Father Meeker," and pressured them to give up their way of life and become obedient Christian farmers. He ignored warnings that the attitude of the Utes toward him was transforming from mild amusement to hatred. The real trouble began when Meeker plowed a favorite horse-racing field of the local Utes. After a confrontation with a Ute leader, he sent for help from Fort Steele in Wyoming. The commander, Major Thomas Thornburgh, set out with between 150 and 200 soldiers. Before they arrived at the agency, they were met by a group of Utes who proposed a meeting, saying they would allow 5 soldiers onto their land. Thornburgh ignored the request, and the troops moved into Ute territory.

Meanwhile, fifty miles away, Utes attacked the agency, killing Meeker and ten other employees. Meeker's wife and daughter were kidnapped, along with two other women. They were released several weeks later, with assistance from Chief Ouray and Chipeta. At least two of the women, including Meeker's Oberlin-educated daughter, Josephine, had been raped.

When Thornburgh and his troops were about twenty miles from the agency, at a place called Milk Creek, they encountered a party of Utes, and a battle ensued. About twenty Utes were killed; Thornburgh and thirteen soldiers were also killed. A subsequent investigation concluded that both Thornburgh and his men and the group of Utes had taken the same trail to avoid the other,[149] with disastrous results.

Chief Ouray and Chipeta were devastated by the news. They correctly understood that their enemies among the Anglos would use this as an excuse to expel the Utes from Colorado. Already ill from nephritis and other health problems, Ouray traveled with Chipeta to Washington to testify about the Meeker Massacre, although the Uncompaghre band was not involved. Chief Ignacio of the Weeminuche band also went on the trip.

Chief Ignacio went to Washington with Ouray and Chipeta, hoping to control the damage done by the Meeker Massacre. *Courtesy Library of Congress.*

Despite these attempts to undo the damage, cries had already risen to a crescendo for the removal of the Utes. Even famed road builder Otto Mears, a longtime friend of the Utes, began calling for their removal. David F. Day, who later served as a Ute agent, also published numerous anti-Ute columns.

Chief Ouray died in August 1880, almost a year after the Meeker Massacre. Within a year of Ouray's death, the Northern Ute bands were forcibly removed from Colorado to Utah. As they left, homesteaders lined up to move in to the vacated territory.

Chipeta lived on, making a meager living as a speaker. According to Jocknick, "Today Chipeta is living among the poorest and most distressed of her tribe, unknown and unsung save in a little poem by Eugene Field at the time of her brave acts."[150] She died in 1924 in Utah and was buried there in Ute fashion. Her body was later moved to the small farm she and Ouray had shared in Montrose, which is now the Ute Indian Museum.

Unlike the Northern Utes, many Southern Utes managed to stay in Colorado. Chief Ignacio of the Weeminuche, along with the Mouache and Capote bands, moved onto the Southern Ute reservation south of Durango.

The year 1887 saw the passage of the Dawes Act, whose purpose was to break up tribal reservations into household allotments of 160 acres for each family head. This would help the Anglo aim to sever tribal loyalties and allow unclaimed land to be purchased by white settlers. Chief Ignacio was among those who refused to go along with the allotment scheme, so he and his band moved to what is today the Ute Mountain Reservation.

After the death of Ouray, a Capote Ute named Sapiah began representing the Utes in dealing with the Anglos. Nicknamed Buckskin Charlie, he learned English and proved a canny negotiator. In 1902, the *Durango Herald* apparently missed the irony when reporting a quote from Buckskin Charlie:

> *The Indians who are attending the district court are creating quite a lot of amusement for those who know how to talk to them. Someone asked Buckskin Charlie if he were a chief, and he answered that he was a chief of a ditch. When he was asked how old he was he couldn't remember how many years he had lived.*[151]

In 1899, unclaimed land in the Southern Ute reservation was opened up for Anglo settlement. Whites were able to purchase lots from the tribe. Half

Buckskin Charlie, who negotiated with the Anglos after Ouray's death, apparently had an ironic sense of humor. *Courtesy Library of Congress.*

a million acres was sold to homesteaders in this fashion. By then, many Utes were living in small houses built by the government and had become farmers or raised cattle, sheep or goats. Game was no longer plentiful, so most were dependent on annuities.

What followed was decades of poverty—but also of hard-won victories. Eventually, the Utes won multimillion-dollar judgments and began to understand and manage their own gas, mineral and water rights. These holdings eventually changed everything for the Southern Utes. As it turned out, they were "sitting on one of the richest gas fields in the country."[152] The "ditch" that Buckskin Charlie referred to turned out to be a very valuable ditch indeed.

Chapter 10

The Wild and Wonderful Circle Route Stage

Early in Colorado's history, the state's boosters were already thinking of ways to attract tourists. An important part of this effort was the "Great Scenic Route," a thousand-mile transportation system that made a loop through some of the prettiest areas in the state. Also referred to as the "circle route," it started out as a train route and later developed into a highway system that is still in use today:

> Starting from Denver, the circle route extends over Lookout mountain to Idaho Springs, Berthoud pass, Kremmling, Walcott, along the Grand to Glenwood Springs, Grand Junction, Delta, Montrose, Ouray, Silverton, Durango, Pagosa Springs, Wolf Creek pass, San Luis valley, Salida, Canon City and Colorado Springs, completing the circle in Denver.[153]

In the early days of the circle route, at least one significant gap existed, through an area that was just too rugged to be tamed. This was the precarious, hair-raising road between Ouray and Red Mountain, built by famed Colorado road-builder Otto Mears back in the 1880s. A train called the Rainbow ran from Silverton to Red Mountain and, at some point, extended into Ironton, but for many years, there was still a missing link into Ouray. One of the last stagecoach companies to fill this gap was an indomitable, well-beloved Ouray company called the Circle Route Stage.

The company advertised themselves as the "Shortest—Cheapest, most picturesque route on earth."[154] In 1904, newspaper ads indicated that the stage left Ouray at 7:30 a.m., arriving at Red Mountain at 10:30 a.m. Today a ghost town located off Highway 550, Red Mountain once boasted a population in the thousands.

National Geographic magazine, in a 1905 feature about the Ouray area, described the Circle Route Stage:

> *One of the very few old overland stage coaches now left in the West runs daily between Ouray and Red Mountain. Its route makes the closing link of 10 miles, through a country inaccessible to the railroad, in the famous "Around the Circle Route" of 1,000 miles, which is made wholly in the*

A woman in 1897 sits in her buggy on the Ouray-Silverton toll road, which is sometimes called the Otto Mears Toll Road. *Courtesy Library of Congress.*

Wicked Tales from Ouray, San Juan and La Plata Counties

A stage between Ouray and Red Mountain, probably the Circle Route Stage, in 1901. *Courtesy Library of Congress.*

state of Colorado. Much of the stage road is cut from nearly vertical rock midway on the flank of a huge mountain at a cost, in places, of nearly $50,000 a mile. To travel along this road on the top of a stage drawn by six horses at a trot—"two in the tongue, two in the swing, and two in the lead"—gazing alternately into dizzy depths below and lofty heights above, is to have an experience that is never forgotten.[155]

The Circle Route Stage Company began operating sometime around 1894, with a six-horse Concord stage coach. In wintertime, to continue delivering mail, freight and passengers, they often had to switch from Concord coaches to sleighs, also pulled by teams of six horses. When

A 1913 view of the famous Concord stagecoach, favored by the Circle Route and other stagecoach companies. *Courtesy Library of Congress.*

conditions got really bad, they resorted to that brawny champion of the San Juans, the pack mule.

The train between Silverton and Red Mountain often became inoperable during the winter, and the trusty Circle Route Stage took over. At other times, the train and stagecoach ran in competition with each other. In 1901, a transportation war boiled, pitting the railroad against the stage in competition for tourist dollars. The *Ouray Plaindealer* revealed their bias with this jab at the "Silverton & Narrow Escape railroad":

> *A railroad and stage rate war is on in the San Juan country...The decision in this struggle rests with the tourists who have thus far shown their preference for the cool airy stage, with its observation perch on the upper deck, to cramped, dusty quarters—with cinder bath included—on the Silverton & Narrow Escape railroad. The commodious stage of the Circle Route conveys passengers to Red Mountain, from which point like daily stage service is available to Silverton.*[156]

In another article, the *Plaindealer* quoted an irate tourist after his train trip, this time dubbed the "Rainbow and Rust railroad": "In the future I'll take the stage or walk. This riding on the eyebrows of a mountain with an insurance policy in one hand and a prayer book in the other is simply a mild form of imbecility."[157]

The San Juans were already famous among adventuresome tourists who came for the stunning scenery and thrills of alpine dangers. The *Ouray Herald* took great delight in describing one such Chicago tourist who had taken the Circle Route Stage from Red Mountain into Ouray:

> *The dizzy heights, the yawning chasms and the weird and wonderful grandeur of the scenery had temporarily imbalanced him and all kinds of wheels were running in opposite directions in his head. Opie* [the tourist] *wears his hair long and each particular hair still stood on end like the quills of a fretful porcupine.*[158]

Driving the bulky six-horse rigs was a harrowing job, particularly in winter when ice patches and snow slides were a constant threat. On February 7, 1902, the afternoon stage did not arrive in Ouray until after midnight because they were stranded by a snowslide at Mother Cline hill. A "snow brigade" had to travel up and dig them out.

Later the same month, another "small slide" occurred on Mother Cline hill as the stage passed through. Early reports said that the horses tumbled "some distance" down an embankment, but there were "only a few passengers and no serious bruises or injuries." Local newspapers were endlessly lighthearted about these dangers, urging readers not to "allow this notice of a little spill to the Circle Route stage to prey upon the fears of your imagination."[159]

The next day, the details of the accident provided in the *Silverton Standard* sounded a lot more serious, though the story was buried on page three: "[The] sleigh, containing eight persons, slipped off the icy road over an embankment and went down the mountain side pell mell for a distance of 300 feet but...no one was injured, not even the horses had been hurt."[160]

Shortly after the accident, the road was closed by snowslides for a month. Somehow intrepid freighters got the mail through to Ironton and Red Mountain using horses and mules, even though the snow was reported to be piled ninety feet high.

An 1882 stagecoach emerges from an early "Riverside Snow Tunnel," topped by a crowd of intrepid tourists—both men and women. *Courtesy Library of Congress.*

That April, a few blizzards later, a company was contracted to dig a snow tunnel to open the route. This was not the first tunnel they had dug at the spot known as Riverside since the road was built. Local boosters, not willing to let a perfectly good snowslide go to waste, advertised the Riverside tunnel as a tourist attraction. The boosters had high hopes for the tunnel:

> *It will be a great sight for the thousands of tourists the railroads have booked for this section of country this season, from the torrid regions of the east, to whom the sight of a huge snow bank in the summer time will be worth hundreds of miles of travel to them, and will be among the most pleasant recollections after they return to their homes.*[161]

Wicked Tales from Ouray, San Juan and La Plata Counties

That August, a Reverend and Mrs. H.A. Ott visiting from Kansas traveled through the San Juans, collecting stories for the reverend's career as a speaker at Chautauquas. He was thrilled to include recollections of the Circle Route Stage and Riverside tunnel in his speaking tour:

> *They provided us with a carriage and took us up the famous Mears Toll Road to Red Mountain, up Uncompahgre canon. Such a wild carriage ride baffles pen to picture. For miles one rides on a shelf of quartzite blasted out of the mountain side, down which he gazes a thousand feet into the bounding, leaping Uncompahgre, and up which he gazes three thousand feet upon hoary cliffs melting into the snowbanks and gnarled timberless summits above. After a six mile drive we found ourselves abreast a great snow-bank. Two great avalanches had descended into the canon last winter filling it up to a depth of fifty feet. The river had tunneled its own way through its depths below and the stage line had tunneled a highway through the icy mass above, and these tunnels were still intact, and into the latter we soon rode amid dripping waters from a thousand melting inverted pinnacles, and chilled by a veritable cold storage. We walked over its summit and gathered a great bouquet of Colorado's state flower, the Columbine, growing at the very brink of the snow gulch.*[162]

Another accident occurred on the circle route on November 4, 1902. The stage, traveling from Red Mountain to Ouray, was coming down a steep grade near a place called Scale's milk ranch. The stagecoach's brakes, which keep the stage from crowding the "wheel horse," became overheated. The horses spooked and began running. Several passengers on the outside of the stage panicked and tumbled over the driver, knocking him off his seat. He lost control of the horses. The stage went off the road and crashed a hundred feet down the mountain.

Fifteen people were on the stage; all were injured, but miraculously, no one was killed. Worst off was a Pueblo businessman, E.C. Mattes, who jumped off and was run over by the stage. One leg was broken in three places; the other broken in one place.

The Circle Route Stage owner, Art Stewart, quickly sent other rigs up to bring the injured down to town. Everyone was bruised and cut, and a number of folks were hospitalized. Several suffered broken limbs and at least a few were in the hospital for some weeks. One horse was killed, and the coach was totaled.

The following June 13, 1903, a rainy day, the stage once again suffered an accident on its way into Ouray. The driver was going downhill at a slow pace when he hit a section of ice. The hind wheels of the carriage slid violently on the ice, causing a king bolt to break. This "detach[ed] the coach from the front wheels, leaving them, horses and driver, still on the road,"[163] while the carriage and its contents went over the cliff and tumbled down 150 to 250 feet. The drop included a 10-foot wall of cribbing. Luckily, the carriage landed in a big pile of snow, which softened the blow. By another miracle, all six passengers survived, though two were seriously injured.

Harry Hope, an elderly gentleman and former county commissioner, was inside the carriage during the entire tumble to the bottom. He was knocked unconscious. This was "the second time that [Harry] has taken an excursion down that hill against his will,"[164] and the newspaper speculated that he would "now join the agitators in the good roads movement."[165] Another injured party was Mrs. W. Lyle, who hurt her back in the fall. Mr. Lyle, also in the accident, would later play a small but notable role in the history of this road.

The resident doctor of the stage company, Dr. Hamilton Fish, was on scene within an hour and a half, tending to the injured who were carried to a Mr. Loneyson's at the Yankee Girl mine. The coach was totaled.

Another accident occurred on October 30, 1907, again while the coach was heading down the hill near the milk ranch, just a half mile outside Ouray. The brakes failed, and the coach bumped up against the horses, which started them on a run. A line to one of the leading horses broke, and the driver couldn't slow them. The horses swerved, and the coach overturned, making two somersaults with ten people aboard. Several leapt from the stage. The driver got a nasty kick in the leg when he tried to untangle one of the horses. Several passengers were seriously injured. In critical condition was the Reverend Baird Mitchell of Durango, whose chest was crushed when the coach landed on him. One of the horses ran all the way into Ouray, which signaled to townspeople that there was a problem up the road. The coach was totaled.

The first years of the twentieth century were a boom time for the tourist trade in the region, and plenty of noise was heard about a new railroad

Wicked Tales from Ouray, San Juan and La Plata Counties

between Ouray and Red Mountain. However, other changes were coming to the region. By 1911, appropriations were being discussed to build a scenic highway through the San Juans between Ouray, Silverton and Durango. In July of that year, the *Ouray Plaindealer* carried a story about Mr. Lyle, who became the first person to ride a motorcycle on the road from Ouray to Silverton. Four years earlier, Mr. Lyle and his wife had been passengers in the stage accident on the same road.[166]

Meanwhile, the faithful old Circle Route Stage continued its runs from Ouray to Red Mountain. Another accident occurred January 9, 1912, this time with the wintertime's Circle Route Stage sleigh. Four horses were pulling the driver and one passenger, and the sleigh was loaded with mail. At the Riverside slide area, they came to a bend in the road, and the sleigh slipped. The whole rig tumbled down one hundred feet into the creek at the bottom of the canyon. The two men jumped off. Two of the horses were killed in the crash, while the other two sustained minor injuries.

A week later the route was closed due to a big snowstorm and more snowslides. The indomitable Circle Route Stage folks headed up on mules and dug out the road. Winter wasn't yet finished with them, however, and March brought fresh blizzards and avalanches. They still managed to get

In the early days, mules were the most reliable means of transportation in the San Juans. *Courtesy Library of Congress.*

the mail through by means of the Circle Route Stage's secret weapon, an infamous mule fondly known as Maude.

Already celebrated in the region for her legendary stamina, Maude gained further notoriety that April when an unfortunate horse had the gall to touch her as they passed each other on the narrow trail. Maude, on the inside as they passed, butted the horse, and it tumbled down into the canyon, where it languished in deep snow until it was rescued following day.

In 1913, newspaper ads for the Circle Route Stage Company and Circle Route Livery transformed into ads for the "Circle Route Garage": "Don't Walk, Ride: When you can taste the incomparable pleasures of a joy ride in a magnificent New Auto at a nominal cost."[167]

Despite the arrival of the automobile, the horse-drawn stage and sleigh were still used for many years after as the most reliable means to keep the mail and passenger traffic moving back and forth through the rough winters. By 1915, construction of the state road along the scenic circle route was well on its way. Ironically, in the 1920s, when the weather got bad, the only way to get gasoline into Silverton was the old reliable horse team.

Chapter 11
"White-Capping" in the San Juans

Of all the folks who voluntarily immigrated to North America in the frontier days, no groups were more vilified and abused than the Chinese and Japanese. Those who made their way to Colorado were not spared. In 1880, a Denver mob rampaged through the Chinese section of town, burning it to the ground and killing at least one man. In 1902, a Chinese man in Idaho Springs was briefly strung up and then run out of town as punishment for his relationship with a white woman. The towns of Aspen and Delta also had incidents of mobs forcibly evicting Chinese businessmen and laborers. In Victor, Colorado, near Cripple Creek, the Victor Fuel Company shut down a coal mine because white miners refused to work with Chinese and Japanese. The fuel company protested that there weren't enough miners and that they needed 20 percent more for their labor force, saying they employed eighteen thousand men but had jobs for fifty thousand.[168]

While all this was going on, the United States Senate passed a series of extensions to the Chinese Exclusion Act. The original 1882 bill made it extremely difficult for Chinese laborers and miners to enter the country for ten years. The bill was extended in 1892 and again in 1902. Provisions added with the extensions disallowed Chinese residents from reentering the country if they left. The 1902 extensions were open-ended and further required all Chinese to register and obtain a certificate of residence. Those

During the 1880 anti-Chinese riot in Denver, rioters beat Chinese residents and destroyed their property. *Courtesy Library of Congress.*

"How our Streets will look next Summer as the result of the Chinese invasion." A dire warning about how Chinese immigrants will displace women in society. *Courtesy Library of Congress.*

who didn't faced deportation. These laws were promptly signed by President Teddy Roosevelt.

Anti-Chinese sentiment came to a head in the San Juan region in 1902, when union men in Silverton raised a boycott of Chinese laundries and restaurants. The Cooks & Waiters Union 16 explained their position in the *Silverton Standard* with a lengthy racist rant, which eventually hit on the familiar crux of the matter: "No white man can compete with their labor on account of their cheapness in living."[169]

The boycott escalated to a point where the Chinese residents—many of whom ran restaurants and laundries—were run out of town. Word of the event reached officials in Washington, D.C., and a week later, Colorado governor James B. Orman received a communiqué from U.S. secretary of state John Hay:

> *It is represented that Chinese residents, about seventy in number, have been ordered to leave Silverton, under threats of violence. An appeal has been made through the Chinese minister for their protection. The department will be pleased if you would take such action as you may find necessary for the protection of the rights of these persons, their business and property.*[170]

Despite these efforts from outside the region, locals were determined:

> *A peaceable arrangement was made today with the Celestials whereby they all agree to sell out their laundries and restaurants before the first of the month and depart from Silverton forever.*
>
> *This is understood to be the beginning of the general retirement of Asiatics from all over Colorado in response to the demands of organized white labor and the wishes of people generally.*[171]

Foremost among the anti-Asian forces were the labor unions. William D. Haywood, secretary of the Western Federation of Miners, sent an op-ed to the *Denver Post*, reprinted in the *Durango Democrat*:

> *If congress does not pass an exclusion act that includes Japanese as well as Chinese the labor organizations, particularly in the great west, will rise up in their might and solve the question for themselves…It is a deplorable state*

of affairs when the homes of thousands of free-born white men are to be jeopardized by a handful of yellow foreigners.[172]

Regional newspaper editors all seemed to agree with organized labor in editorial condemnations of the "Celestials," such as this comment from the *Ouray Plaindealer*: "Drive out the Japs and Chinese. If the trusts and money lords who make the laws of this country are bound to oppress American labor with cheap Asiatic importations, let the white workman retaliate by taking a club to every saffron-hued peon that sticks his head over the breastworks."[173]

A number of the Chinese and Japanese who'd been evicted from Silverton moved on to Ouray or Durango. The result was a boycott of Chinese and Japanese businesses in those towns. In March, the courthouse in Ouray was packed with the town's men and women, all present to "discuss the question of peacefully bringing about such a condition of affairs that would remove the Chinese and Japanese from the vicinity."[174] The discussion at the meeting followed the usual line of objection made against ethnic groups: the Chinese sent their earnings back to China, they did not assimilate, their "method of living" was un-American. The *Ouray Plaindealer* again hit on the crux of the matter: despite the fact that "this class of people seldom caused disturbances...[they] interfered with the possibilities of...white labor."[175]

Secretary of State John Hay soon sent another message to Governor Orman, saying exactly the same thing, except naming Ouray instead of Silverton.

In early May 1902, the previously peaceful boycotts and evictions turned violent in Silverton. Apparently hoping that the furor had died down, about a dozen Chinese returned to Silverton the first week of May. There they quietly reopened a laundry and connected restaurant called the O.K. Chinese Restaurant.

A few days later, a group of forty anti-Chinese agitators gathered at midnight. They forced their way into the O.K. Restaurant, took two men hostage and robbed them. The newspaper accounts were vague about what happened next, but the Chinese were apparently beaten, tortured and run out of town. The mob next tried to get into the laundry, but the men inside barricaded the place and managed to keep them out.

While this was going on, one clever Chinese man called "Spider" had slipped unnoticed out the back of the O.K. Restaurant. Spider had lived in Silverton for fourteen years. He ran down to the city hall and rang the fire bell. This roused the police and other citizens, who saw what was happening and put a stop to it.

For most citizens, even though they had joined in the general anti-Asian chorus, this brutal act was too extreme. The *Ouray Herald* published an editorial speaking out against the "outrages perpetrated upon the non-resistent [*sic*] residents. To use plain language, the 'white-capping' of the Chinese was a foul outrage and a stain upon the fair name of this community. Every man connected with that circumstance was a law-breaker and worse." [176]

"White-capping" referred to a movement that first emerged during the 1870s that was similar in belief, act and costume to the Ku Klux Klan.

Other newspapers reported that the Chinese had been robbed of hundreds of dollars and were "subjected to stringing up and tortures in way of brutal treatment that should d——n all who lent their aid to such atrocious work."[177] Although he had previously published numerous anti-Chinese editorials, David Day at the *Durango Democrat* now excoriated the mob:

> *The dastardly character of the undertaking had a tendency to reverse all who were against the Chinamen, and they were rapidly placed under police protection with Sheriff Casad and the city officers in charge.*
>
> *During the shameful raid there were seven or eight shots fired, the Chinamen returning the fire and exhibiting no symptoms of fear other than such as the overpowering odds visited upon them.*
>
> *Yesterday three or four of the mob were recognized by their victims, and others had been recognized by parties returning from a social function, at least some of Silverton's people claim to have recognized the voices.*
>
> *Our latest advices are to effect that the Chinese minister in Washington has been wired of the outrage and a bill for damages and money stolen will no doubt be presented and paid.*[178]

Reports varied about how many men were hurt in the attack. Secretary of State Hay received a report that "one had been lost, others badly beaten and the house occupied by one of them broken into and robbed."[179]

One man who had been "escorted" out of town by the mob ended up walking barefooted for thirty miles along the train tracks. He was picked up by the train in a deplorable condition. His clothing had been torn, and his feet were cut, bruised and blistered. Passengers on the train helped him on, paid his fare and, once in Durango, helped him onto a wagon that took him to Chinese friends in that town. The mob had stolen $500 from him.

Even the editors at the *Silverton Standard*, who had used much column space demonizing the Chinese, spoke up against the raid: "The mal-treatment of a dog in such a manner as was meted to the two Chinamen would naturally elicit condemnation from any human being..."[180]

The *Ouray Herald* attempted to paint the issue as a Silverton problem, decrying the "howling, drunken mob [that] assaulted and brutally treated a few defenseless Chinamen, pounding three almost to death, and perhaps killing the one that cannot be found."[181] The *Herald* went further:

> *The reply of the sheriff of San Juan county to Governor Orman, that everything was quiet and that no further trouble was anticipated, is a plain indication that the people of Silverton are trying to smother it. All reports go to show that if the authorities were not in full sympathy with the mob that they intended to whitewash the whole thing if possible.*
>
> *The Chinamen were abused worse than any humane man would abuse a burro, three of them shamefully pounded up, some doubts being expressed as to their recovery.*[182]

Not surprisingly, the *Silverton Standard* shot back against the *Ouray Herald*, bringing up the lynching of the Cuddigans and the "burning alive of a Negro," which the newspaper claimed took place in Ouray.[183]

A "law and order league" was formed in Silverton to prevent future attacks, but the Chinese were still not welcome in town.

Chapter 12
Tragedy at Pine River

Ludwig Mountain is a beautiful rise in a bucolic valley north of Bayfield, northeast of the spot where Bear Creek joins the Pine River. North of the mountain is Wommer Draw. In the summer of 1916, this area was the scene of what the *Bayfield Blade* called the "worst tragedy in Pine River's history."[184]

Henry Ludwig was one of the earliest settlers in the valley of the Pine River, also called Los Piños. After emigrating from Germany in 1875, he married and moved to the San Juan region in the early 1880s. He worked as a miner for a time and also ran a newspaper at Animas Forks. In the mid-1880s, he and his wife, Emma, began operating their ranch at the mouth of Bear Creek.

The Ludwigs shared rights to a ditch with their neighbors, the Wommers and the Lowells. The three families and other local farmers had long cooperated out of necessity in this remote region. The Wommers had emigrated from Germany in the late 1860s. Two of the Ludwig girls, Rosa and Hattie, had married two of the Wommer boys, Louis and Frank, respectively. Relative latecomers, the Lowells moved to Colorado from the Cherokee Nation reservation in Indian Territory (Oklahoma) in the early 1900s.

By all accounts, Henry Ludwig was an angry fellow. Newspapers described him as *possessed of a very mean temper and would fly into a rage under the slightest provocation, yet he was about 66 years old and never before got into any very serious trouble, although he had threatened members of his family many times. He was unreasonable in nearly all things. Wherever he went he nearly always packed a gun of some kind.*[185]

The trouble began on a July day in 1916. That morning, Henry Ludwig marched over to the shared ditch and closed the outlet that led to the Lowell ranch, running the water to his own ranch. The spot was "just east of the county road and east of the Lowell residence."[186] Sixteen-year-old Frank Lowell came by, taking his horses to pasture. He saw what was going on and confronted Ludwig about the water.

The families had an agreement that they would share the water and the ditch maintenance, but that year Ludwig had failed to help clean and repair the ditch. According to their agreement, this meant he forfeited his rights to the water. Ludwig apparently didn't like being reminded of this by the lad. An argument ensued and quickly escalated to a shouting match.

In the nearby Lowell house, Frank's father, Abner Lowell, heard the ruckus. Recovering from a broken leg, he picked up a shotgun and hobbled out to the ditch, accompanied by his other son, eighteen-year-old Hugh. Ludwig heard the others coming and quickly left, hiding in a bank of bushes. There, apparently expecting trouble, he had previously stashed a 45-60 Winchester rifle. When Abner and Hugh Lowell arrived, Ludwig opened fire from the bushes, hitting Abner Lowell in the hip. Abner fell, and Ludwig shot him once more, the bullet hitting him in the chest.

Hugh ran to his fallen father, calling out to Ludwig to stop firing. Ludwig then shot Hugh Lowell in the head, killing him instantly. Ludwig still wasn't finished. He shot Frank, wounding him in the hip.

Still alive, Abner Lowell fired his shotgun into the bushes from where the gunshots were coming, but Ludwig had made his escape.

In all, Ludwig fired six shots, and four of those hit a Lowell.

Mrs. Lowell and other neighbors arrived quickly on the scene and carried Abner and the deceased Hugh into the Lowell ranch house. Law enforcement and a doctor were notified, and a *Bayfield Blade* reporter accompanied them to the home. The doctor went to work on Abner and Frank. Abner was gravely wounded, with a bullet in his lung and another in his intestines. He managed to tell the story to Justice of the Peace Frederic Jephcott and the reporter. Two hours later, forty-eight-year-old Abner Lowell died of his injuries.

Only young Frank Lowell survived the event. Forty-five-year-old Ruth Lowell was left to bury her husband and teenage son. She was now a widow with three children to care for on her own: sixteen-year-old Frank, eleven-year-old Hilda and eight-year-old Arthur.

Justice Jephcott notified officials in Durango and waited for their arrival before going after Henry Ludwig. At midafternoon, four officers arrived: Sheriff Arthur Fassbinder; District Attorney George Lane and a deputy; and the deputy coroner, George Goodman. The sheriff quickly formed a posse, and they headed out to the Ludwig ranch house. They surrounded the place and called for Henry Ludwig to come out.

Soon, Mrs. Emma Ludwig came alone out of the house. She informed DA Lane that her husband was inside, armed with a rifle, revolver and shotgun. Henry Ludwig had declared he would not be taken alive. She said Henry claimed he hadn't meant to kill young Hugh Lowell.

After some discussion, and at great risk to his own safety, George Lane began walking toward the house with Emma. He hoped to convince Ludwig to surrender peacefully. As they approached, they heard a muffled gunshot from inside the house. Emma Ludwig ran inside, then soon emerged and beckoned to Lane and the others. When the men entered, they found a room filled with gunpowder smoke. Ludwig sat limply in a rocking chair. He had apparently rested his Winchester on the floor and leaned over it, firing a bullet into his own chest. He was dead.

He left behind his widow, two sons, four daughters and numerous grandchildren.

The fallout from this tragedy was not over. In late August, six weeks after the shootings, Henry Ludwig's daughter, Mrs. Hattie Wommer, suffered a breakdown. She was taken to a hospital in Durango where she was treated for a "deranged mind."[187] Within a week, she was "adjudged insane" in the county court[188] and taken away to the state asylum, accompanied by her sister, eighteen-year-old Ruby Ludwig, and Mr. and Mrs. Arthur Fassbinder.

Postscript

Despite the devastation the shootings wreaked on the three families who shared the little creek, folks eventually recovered. The 1920 census shows the Pine River clans going on with their lives (not to mention a plethora of Franks): Hattie Ludwig Wommer was back at home with her husband, Frank, and her son, Frank Jr. Henry Ludwig's widow, Emma, moved in with her son, Frank, and his family. Ruth Lowell moved to Hesperus where she managed the post office there. Her son, the injured Frank, lived with her and worked as a clerk at the post office. Together, they cared for Arthur and Hilda.

Chapter 13

The Sheriff and Marshal Shoot It Out

On a cold January day in 1906, the quiet winter streets of Durango were jarred by a shootout between two men. Unfortunately, witnesses had trouble calling for help because the shooters were Durango's deputy marshal Jesse C. Stansel and La Plata County sheriff William J. Thompson.

The shooting erupted during an argument over the enforcement of Durango's antigambling laws. For several months, Sheriff Thompson had been working to shut down gambling facilities in Durango, which still operated despite its prohibition. The night before, Thompson had raided the El Moro saloon, which meant he confiscated a roulette wheel and told proprietor John Hartman he needed to appear in court to face gambling charges. Just before the shooting, Thompson had been inside the same saloon accusing Hartman of "running a gambling house for Wickline and that [Hartman] was paying the police."[189] The Wickline mentioned was William "Billy" Wickline, Durango's city marshal, who was also reportedly part owner of the El Moro saloon. El Moro was used as an unofficial police station, as the department did not yet have one.

Thompson then went outside and berated Deputy Stansel for not enforcing the laws against gambling. According to witness David B. Hayes: "Thompson said to Stansel: 'You know all about this gambling.' Stansel replied: 'I am under orders from the marshal and city council and not you.'

Thompson repeated. Stansel repeated his line of duty. Thompson then said 'G-d d——n you.' Stansel says: 'Don't G-d d——n me.'"[190]

There were about as many versions of what happened next as there were witnesses. One man, W.T. Darlington, said that Thompson fired the first shot:

> *Then Thompson started and walked off four or five steps south, whirled around, pulled his gun and fired. Then they commenced shooting from both sides. They shot until their guns were empty. They both examined their six-shooters and found that they were empty, then they went at each other and beat each other over their heads. Thompson turned and walked to the barber shop door, Stansel turned and walked into the El Moro, shortly returning with a six-shooter in each hand. He saw that Thompson was lying in front of the barber shop, turned and walked back into the El Moro.*[191]

On the other hand, Chas. E. Allen testified that Stansel shot at Thompson as the latter walked away. Thomas Rockwood said both men drew their revolvers at the same time, with Thompson possibly firing first.

As Thompson lay bleeding in the barbershop doorway, his son, George, arrived on scene. Thompson had difficulty speaking but asked if Stansel was in jail. To keep him calm, those around him told him yes. Thompson then looked at his son and said, "The s.o.b. murdered me."[192] He was taken to the Ochsner Hospital but died just as he arrived.

Dr. H.C. Turrell testified at the inquest that Thompson had five gunshot wounds—one in the abdomen, one through the lung, two through the neck that exited out the back and the last through the nostril into his brain. Thompson also had a cut on his right cheek, a bad scalp wound and a gash in the back of the head. His face also showed injuries from a pistol whipping.

Forty-four-year-old Thompson had a wife, Sarah; two daughters, ages ten and seventeen; and three grown sons. He was a pioneer of the region who'd been in the area for twenty-six years. Originally a stockman, he'd been in law enforcement for twelve years.

Thirty-nine-year-old Jesse Stansel was also seriously injured. A .38-caliber ball went through his right collar bone and lodged in his lung. He was taken to Mercy Hospital where doctors were able to remove it. His wife, Ella, stayed by his bed. The Stansels had four sons and a daughter, the youngest child six months old and the eldest fifteen.

During the shootout, an innocent bystander, seventy-two-year-old John Acord, was also shot in the arm. The bullet fractured the bones around his elbow. Doctors at Mercy Hospital had to remove the elderly fellow's arm just below the shoulder.

There was much discussion among townspeople about what had caused the sudden eruption of violence between the two lawmen. Prior to this, there had been no fights or ongoing wars between them. One possible factor soon emerged in the local papers. The *Durango Democrat* published a column suggesting that Thompson had been drinking at the time of the shootout. The *Durango Weekly Banner/Durango Wage Earner* reported that "parties who saw the sheriff last night said he had been drinking excessively and was under the influence of drink…using abusive language to the management of the El Moro."[193] Several others testified that they saw him drinking that morning, although the doctor who performed the post mortem said he detected no odor of alcohol.

Stansel, on the other hand, was not a drinker and claimed that he'd only been drunk twice in his life, when he was a teenager.

A year earlier, Thompson and Stansel had run against each other for sheriff. The campaign had gotten ugly, but the two men had reportedly agreed to put a stop to that:

> *Over zealous friends on both sides started stories on the opposing sides, which were calculated to make men fight, and Thompson went to Stansel and told him he did not want to make such a campaign and they agreed to try to cut out all personalities. After the election was over the two men appeared to get along very well until after Sheriff Thompson tried to close gambling, when he claimed the aid of the police officers in doing this. Thompson made the claim repeatedly that instead of the police helping him they were doing what they could to prevent his closing gambling.*[194]

Two days after the shooting, the county commissioners appointed Thompson's brother, George W. Thompson, as sheriff. The same day, Thompson's funeral was held at Red Men's Hall. All business in town was suspended from one to three in the afternoon while the county paid its last respects to their sheriff. Thompson was buried at Durango's Greenmount Cemetery.

Grave of Sheriff William J. Thompson. *Courtesy Greenmount Cemetery, Durango.*

Meanwhile, as Jesse Stansel recovered at Mercy Hospital, a warrant was issued for his arrest. He hired Willis A. Reese as his attorney. The prosecution consisted of George W. Lane, DA James Pulliam and Charles A. Johnson.

The preliminary hearing was held January 31, during which detailed testimony was taken. Described by the *Durango Democrat* as "the most memorable preliminary trial ever held in La Plata county,"[195] the several dozen people who had witnessed the shootout gave many different accounts of the event. There was much contradictory discussion about who was standing where, who shot first and who had what sort of gun.

Stansel was present at the hearing but "showed evidence of confinement, looking somewhat run down and weak but with all maintained a retired demeanor throughout."[196] The *Durango Democrat* went to some length to express support for Stansel:

> *I want to say that I believe as much as I believe anything that when Thompson turned to leave Stansel he did so to deceive him into belief*

that he was through with him and was going away, intending all the time to pull his gun and turn and shoot him and the only thing that saved Stansel's life was that he stepped back far enough to escape the first shot fired by Thompson.[197]

After the hearing, Stansel was released on $10,000 bond. Jury selection for his trial started on March 29, 1906, and it got underway on April 2. Each side presented essentially the same witnesses who testified at the preliminary hearing. One new witness was John Acord, who was still recovering after losing his arm. He said, "Thompson passed on down the street. I heard a shot, Thompson turned and had a pistol in his hand and before I knew it I was hit. Who shot me I do not know."[198]

Jesse Stansel testified on his own behalf. He said he'd known Thompson since 1892 when he came to the area and had always been on friendly terms with him. The day of the shooting was the first sign of trouble between the two. He was filling in that day for Marshal Wickline:

I first saw Thompson about 10 o'clock, he walked into the Bismarck with another man. Next time I saw him he came out of the Bismarck and passed myself and Wickline, who were talking. I next saw him in the Horseshoe where I went to the toilet…Thompson and I did not speak. I passed out and walked down to the First National bank. On returning I was talking with Asher in front of the El Moro when Thompson went in there. He came and walked up to me, saying: "I guess. G—— d—— you, you don't know about gambling." I replied I knew as much about it as he did. I told him to cut out the G—— d—— part as I would not stand for it and to treat me as a gentleman and I would treat him as such. He then stepped away and looking back sort of sideways, said: "Maybe you are looking for something?" I replied, "No, I am not." He whirled with drawn gun and said: "Well, if you are, I will give it to you, you s.o.b." and fired. I had my right hand in my overcoat pocket and left hand in my pants pocket. We were three or four feet apart. Then we worked together. He placed his gun at my abdomen and I knocked his hand away as he fired. I shot him in the side at this time. Thompson shot four times. The gun in evidence looks like my gun. After my gun was empty I started to reload and Thompson came toward me with raised gun to strike, and did strike me on the shoulder.

I struck him five or six times. I did not hear anyone call to me to stop. I went into the El Moro and I think it was Hartman gave me another gun. I went out and seeing Thompson laying on the sidewalk I then called to someone to get me a doctor as I was hurt seriously. It was the second shot from Thompson's gun that struck me in the chest. I shot at Thompson to keep him from killing me.[199]

When both sides rested their cases, the court gave instructions to the jury, saying they could either convict Stansel of first-degree murder or acquit him.

The jury came back with a verdict of not guilty.

Despite his acquittal, many in town called for Jesse Stansel's removal from the police force. However, Jesse was soon back at work with "that star on his left breast."

That fall, William Thompson's brother George ran for sheriff of La Plata County on the antigambling platform. His opponent was John Clark (or Clarke). The *Durango Democrat* went after Thompson in a long-winded attack,[200] using as many words as possible to say he'd been lax about gambling since taking over for his fallen brother. The editorial included a long rant in all capital letters, asking what happened to the notorious roulette wheel that William Thompson had confiscated prior to the shooting.

Ever on the opposing side, the *Durango Wage Earner* urged folks to vote for George Thompson.

Clark won the election.

Postscript

Within a couple of years, Jesse Stansel left the area with his family and moved to El Paso, Texas, where he and his wife ran a rooming house. The 1930 census describes Jesse Stansel of El Paso as a private detective.

John Acord died in 1914, having never quite recovered from ongoing troubles caused by the loss of his arm.

Chapter 14

The High Price of Being (and Killing) a Gentleman

Born in 1850 New York, Thomas Greatorex was an early and prominent pioneer of the San Juan region. He was said to have friends in "every town in San Juan."[201] As a young man back east, he had worked as a page in the House of Representatives. In 1875, he headed west to Del Norte where he worked as a clerk of the district court. A year later, Greatorex moved to Silverton where he once again served as clerk and recorder for the town. In 1878, together with the famed Otto Mears and several others, Greatorex formed a local "Bell Telephone" company in Saguache, organizing the first telephone line between Saguache and Del Norte. In 1880, the Silverton census lists his occupation as "real estate." He also served as abstract clerk of San Juan County.

Described as "always quiet, always gentlemanly, always jolly" and a man of "high breeding and polished gentility,"[202] Thomas Greatorex came from an extraordinary family populated by highly accomplished women. His mother, Eliza, was a famous sketch artist. Born in Ireland in 1819, Eliza Pratt Greatorex was an educated woman who immigrated with her family to New York in 1836. There she attended art school. In 1849, she married Henry Wellington Greatorex, a well-known organist and composer still remembered today for his hymn music, including, "Gloria Patri." The couple had three children: Kathleen, Elizabeth and Thomas.

The Greatorex family traveled widely, as Henry made musical tours until his sudden death in 1858. The widow then settled in New York with her three youngsters. She supported the family by selling her work, teaching art and publishing books of her sketches. She and her sister, the writer Matilda Despard, created a travel book together called *Old New York from the Battery to Bloomingdale*. Eliza's work hangs in prominent museums, and her sketches of New York City scenes are among her most famous.

The family headed back to Europe in 1861, living in Paris and Munich. In the 1870s, they returned to the States, where Eliza received a commission to go to Colorado and make etchings of the mountain scenery. The family packed up again and moved to Colorado Springs. The result of Eliza's work there was the 1873 book *Summer Etchings in Colorado*, which she dedicated to the "Fountain Colony," the original name given to Colorado Springs by General William J. Palmer in 1871.

After Colorado, Eliza and her daughters headed back east and on to Europe and North Africa. However, Thomas apparently decided that he couldn't leave the place where, as his mother described in her book, "we

Mother of Thomas, Eliza Greatorex was a well-known artist specializing in etchings and sketches, like this drawing of Mont St. Michel in Brittany. *Courtesy Library of Congress.*

found beauty indescribable—grandeur unimaginable."²⁰³ Instead of going back with his mother and sisters, he separated from them and headed on his own farther into the untamed west.

There, unfortunately, this worldly and accomplished man's own sense of gallantry eventually got him into deep trouble.

The problem began in the wee morning hours of March 8, 1881, in Durango. At three o'clock in the morning, two couples were among the audience at the Coliseum auditorium. When the entertainment ended, the two young ladies, Mabel Young and Alice Haskell, began quarreling. The girls were soon fighting and pulling each other's hair. Their two male companions, Tom Lynch and Jack Roberts, jumped into the fight, creating a brawling foursome.

Thomas Greatorex was also in the audience and had lingered after the end of the show. He saw the brawl and, feeling that the ladies might be at risk, jumped in to rescue them. Jack Roberts pulled out a revolver and clobbered Greatorex on the head. As Greatorex fell to the ground, Roberts shot him in the back at point-blank range. The bullet entered at the base of the spine, traveling downward through the sacrum. The muzzle was so close to his body, his clothing was burned.

Durango marshal Heathey, also trying to stop the disturbance, was severely injured when he was bashed in the head with a revolver. He didn't see who struck the blow.

Jack Roberts fled the place through a side door and disappeared into the dark. Two doctors were called, Dr. Plumb and Dr. Clay. Greatorex was first laid out on a table, where he was still alive but bleeding profusely. The doctors had him carried to a private office at the San Juan Lumber Company on Railroad Street where they tried to keep him alive.

Meanwhile, with Jack Roberts on the run, rumblings began in the region. As described in the *Dolores News*, "Mr. Greatorex has friends who are numbered only by the population of the San Juan, and the unexpected calamity which has befallen him has caused each of them to pray for his recovery as though he were a brother."²⁰⁴ Officials offered a $500 reward for Jack Roberts, dead or alive.

After a couple weeks of agony and rising and falling hopes for his recovery, Thomas Greatorex died of his injuries. Durango businesses shut down during his funeral, which was attended by many. The newspaper reported that he was buried "in private grounds across the river, pending the wishes of his relatives."[205] His mother and sisters were reportedly in Algiers at the time of Thomas's death and were said to be on their way to Durango.

In a fond eulogy, the *Dolores News* wrote:

> *We often see those who endeavor to be gentlemen from force of circumstances and for appearances' sake, but seldom one who is such in following the dictates of a noble soul. Such a man it was of whom we write today. Generous in spirit, kind of heart, manly in demeanor, strong in mind and jolly in companionship, he was admired in his daily life. An excellent singer, an accomplished dancer, graceful in carriage, handsome in face and figure and engaging in conversation, he was the life of society and an indispensable addition to every gathering."*[206]

Greatorex was also eulogized in a *New York Times* column, which was reprinted by other papers:

> *Greatorex was a New Yorker and had many warm friends here, who will be pained and shocked to learn of his sudden taking-off. He had been five years in Colorado, where he was much esteemed, and had filled various important offices. Those who knew him say that he was of a noble disposition; that he had always esteemed and reverenced women and was quick to resent any insult or injury done to them.*[207]

While Durango's citizens mourned their fallen friend, news arrived that Jack Roberts had been captured somewhere to the south. The dispatch said that his captors wanted to turn him over to authorities at Cox's ranch and would collect the $500 reward there. Upon this news, forty men mounted up and headed south, carrying the reward money with them.

When the men returned to Durango, they had no prisoner with them. They offered little explanation about what happened to Jack Roberts.

The *Dolores News* made this brief report:

> DIED. *On or about March 16th, at some point between the lower line of the Ute reservation and Durango, Colo., one cowardly assassin, known on earth as Jack Roberts. His death resulted from unknown causes, probably from undertaking to balance on the ragged edge of thin air. Funeral services of the deceased will extend over a period of several days, Rev. Drs. Buzzard and Coyote officiating.*[208]

Notes

1. Death of the Secret Service Man

1. Callaghan, "Investigation of Colorado Land Fraud Case."
2. Ibid.
3. *Durango Democrat*, April 28, 1908.
4. *Durango Democrat*, November 5, 1907.
5. Callaghan, "Investigation of Colorado Land Fraud Case."
6. *Telluride Daily Journal*, November 6, 1907.
7. *Durango Democrat*, November 8, 1907.
8. Ibid.
9. Hunter, et al., "Statement."
10. *Durango Democrat*, November 9, 1907.
11. *Durango Wage Earner*, January 2, 1908.
12. Ibid.
13. *Breckenridge Bulletin*, November 9, 1907.
14. Ibid.
15. Ibid.
16. *Durango Wage Earner*, January 2, 1908.
17. *Durango Democrat*, January 9, 1908.
18. Ibid., April 26, 1908.

19. Ibid., April 28, 1908.
20. Ibid.
21. Ibid.
22. Ibid.
23. Ibid.
24. Ibid., April 30, 1908.
25. Ibid., April 28, 1908.
26. *Durango Wage Earner*, April 30, 1908.
27. *Durango Democrat*, April 28, 1908.
28. Ibid.
29. Ibid.
30. Ibid., April 29, 1908.
31. Ibid.
32. Ibid.
33. Ibid.
34. Ibid.
35. Ibid.
36. Ibid., April 30, 1908.
37. Ibid.
38. Ibid.
39. Ibid.
40. Ibid., May 2, 1908.
41. Ibid.
42. Ibid.
43. Ibid.
44. Ibid.
45. Ibid., November 4, 1908.
46. *Durango Wage Earner*, January 7, 1909.
47. Ibid., April 8, 1909.
48. *Colorado Transcript*, August 11, 1910.

2. Bad Blood on Bear Creek

49. *Durango Democrat*, November 17, 1903.
50. *Durango Wage Earner*, January 14, 1904.

51. *The Pacific Reporter*.
52. Ibid.
53. Ibid.
54. Ibid.
55. *Durango Democrat*, September 21, 1905.
56. *Silverton Standard*, September 23, 1905.

3. THE GRAVE MISFORTUNE OF KID ADAMS, THE OURAY HIGHWAYMAN

57. Friedman, Inflation Calculator.
58. *Silverite-Plaindealer*, October 6, 1899.
59. Ibid.
60. *Ouray Herald*, Thursday October 5, 1899.
61. *Silverite-Plaindealer*, October 6, 1899.
62. Ibid., October 13, 1899.
63. Ibid.
64. *Aspen Tribune*, October 17, 1899.
65. Ibid.
66. *Silverite-Plaindealer*, October 20, 1899.
67. *Telluride Daily Journal*, December 6, 1899.
68. *Silverite-Plaindealer*, October 6, 1899.
69. *Ouray Herald*, October 5, 1899.
70. *Silverite-Plaindealer*, October 20, 1899
71. Ibid.

4. DANGEROUS WOMEN

72. *Silverton Standard*, July 27, 1912.
73. *Telluride Daily Journal*, August 24, 1912.
74. *Silverton Standard*, September 28 1912.
75. Ibid.
76. Ibid.

5. Durango Desperadoes

77. Benson, "Port Stockton, Outlaw," 109.
78. *Denver Republican*, June 22, 1879.
79. *Dolores News*, July 10, 1880.
80. Ibid., April 9, 1881.
81. *Leadville Daily Herald*, April 15, 1881.
82. *Dolores News*, April 16, 1881.
83. Ibid., May 28, 1881.
84. Stanley, *The Private War*, 116.
85. *Dolores News*, April 30, 1881.
86. Ibid., May 14, 1881.
87. *Aspen Times*, May 21, 1881.
88. Ibid.
89. Ibid.
90. *Dolores News*, June 4, 1881.
91. Ibid., June 18, 1881.
92. *Helena Independent*, June 28, 1881.
93. *Dolores News*, August 20, 1881.
94. Stanley, *The Private War*, 143.
95. Ibid., 149.
96. *Dolores News*, August 27, 1881.
97. Stanley, *The Private War*, 116.
98. *Dolores News*, September 3, 1881.
99. Ibid., September 10, 1881.
100. Ibid.
101. Stanley, *The Private War*, 124.
102. *Durango Herald*, September 29, 1881.
103. *Dolores News*, October 1, 1881.

6. The Tragic Tale of Mary Rose and the Cuddigans

104. *Dolores News*, January 26, 1884.
105. Ibid.

106. Ibid.
107. *White Pine Cone*, January 25, 1884.
108. *Colorado Transcript*, January 23, 1884.
109. *White Pine Cone*, January 25, 1884.
110. *Leadville Herald*, January 22, 1884.
111. Ibid.
112. Segrave, *Lynchings of Women*, 37.
113. *Rocky Mountain Sun*, March 22, 1884.
114. *Fort Collins Courier*, February 7, 1884.
115. Ibid.
116. *Dolores News*, February 2, 1884.

7. The Famous and the Infamous Days of the San Juans

117. *Saguache Chronicle*, May 4, 1878.
118. *Montezuma Millrun*, December 29, 1883.
119. *Ouray Herald*, January 3, 1901.
120. *Akron Pioneer Press*, May 22, 1903.
121. *Telluride Daily Journal*, May 21, 1903.
122. Ibid.
123. Ibid., April 24, 1922.
124. Ibid.
125. Ibid., April 27, 1922.
126. Ibid.
127. Ibid., December 4, 1922.
128. Ibid., December 8, 1922.
129. Ibid., December 9, 1922.

8. A Colorado Range War

130. *Durango Democrat*, February 24, 1904.
131. *Telluride Daily Journal*, February 6, 1905.
132. *Durango Wage Earner*, February 9, 1905.

133. Ibid., January 5, 1911.
134. Craig, *The Cox-Truby Feud*, 6.
135. *Durango Wage Earner*, June 8, 1911.
136. Craig, *The Cox-Truby Feud*, 29.
137. *Bayfield Blade*, June 8, 1911.
138. Ibid.
139. Ibid., June 15, 1911.
140. Craig, *The Cox-Truby Feud*, 34–35.
141. *Bayfield Blade*, August 24, 1911.
142. Ibid., December 7, 1911.
143. Craig, *The Cox-Truby Feud*, 17–18.
144. *Bayfield Blade*, June 27, 1912.
145. *Ignacio Chieftain*, July 29, 1921.
146. Ibid., January 6, 1922.

9. "THE UTES MUST GO"

147. Marsh, *People of the Shining Mountains*, 64.
148. Jocknick, *Early Days*, 116–17.
149. *New York Times*, December 4, 1879.
150. Jocknick, *Early Days*, 181.
151. *Durango Wage Earner*, August 14, 1902.
152. Thompson, "The Ute Paradox."

10. THE WILD AND WONDERFUL CIRCLE ROUTE STAGE

153. *Silverton Standard*, March 17, 1917.
154. *Durango Democrat*, January 28, 1904.
155. "Maps Recently Published," *National Geographic Magazine*, 423–24.
156. *Ouray Plaindealer*, July 19, 1901.
157. Ibid., August 2, 1901.
158. *Ouray Herald*, December 5, 1901.
159. Ibid., February 21, 1902.

160. *Silverton Standard*, February 22, 1902.
161. *Ouray Herald*, May 16, 1902.
162. Ibid., August 15, 1902.
163. Ibid., June 19, 1903
164. Ibid.
165. Ibid.
166. *Ouray Plaindealer*, July 21, 1911.
167. *Silverton Standard*, July 12, 1913.

11. "White-Capping" in the San Juans

168. *Telluride Journal*, February 20, 1902.
169. *Silverton Standard*, February 8, 1902.
170. Ibid., February 13, 1902.
171. *Telluride Daily Journal*, February 20, 1902.
172. *Durango Democrat*, February 21, 1902.
173. *Ouray Plaindealer*, February 28, 1902.
174. Ibid., March 7, 1902.
175. Ibid.
176. *Ouray Herald*, May 30, 1902.
177. *Durango Democrat*, May 14, 1902.
178. Ibid.
179. *Silverton Standard* May 17, 1902.
180. Ibid.
181. *Ouray Herald*, May 23, 1902.
182. Ibid.
183. *Silverton Standard*, May 31, 1902.

12. Tragedy at Pine River

184. *Bayfield Blade*, July 7, 1916.
185. Ibid.
186. Ibid.

187. Ibid., September 1, 1916.
188. Ibid., September 8, 1916.

13. The Sheriff and Marshal Shoot It Out

189. *Durango Democrat*, January 10, 1906.
190. Ibid.
191. Ibid., January 20, 1906.
192. Ibid., February 1, 1906.
193. *Durango Weekly Banner/Durango Wage Earner*, January 11, 1906.
194. Ibid.
195. *Durango Democrat*, February 3, 1906.
196. Ibid., February 1, 1906.
197. Ibid., February 3, 1906.
198. Ibid., April 3, 1906.
199. Ibid., April 6, 1906.
200. Ibid., October 28, 1906.

14. The High Price of Being (and Killing) a Gentleman

201. *Dolores News*, March 12, 1881.
202. Ibid.
203. Greatorex, *Summer Etchings in Colorado*.
204. *Dolores News*, March 12, 1881.
205. Ibid., March 26, 1881.
206. Ibid.
207. *Logansport Indiana*, April 6, 1881.
208. *Dolores News*, March 26, 1881.

Bibliography

BOOKS

Aldrich, John K. *Ghosts of the Western San Juans, Volume I.* Denver, CO: Columbine Ink, 1997.

———. *Ghosts of the Western San Juans, Volume II.* Denver, CO: Columbine Ink, 1997.

Benham, Jack. *Silverton.* Ouray, CO: Bear Creek Publishing, 1981.

Benson, Maxine. "Port Stockton, Outlaw." *Western Voices: 125 Years of Colorado Writing.* Edited by Ben Fogelberg and Steve Grinstead. Golden, CO: Colorado Historical Society and Fulcrum, 2004.

Craig, Phillip R. *The Cox-Truby Feud.* Flora Vista, NM: San Juan County Historical Society, 2002.

Eberhart, Perry. *Guide to the Colorado Ghost Towns and Mining Camps.* Athens, OH: Swallow Press, 1969.

Greatorex, Eliza. *Summer Etchings in Colorado.* New York: G.P. Putnam's Sons, 1873.

Jocknick, Sidney. *Early Days on the Western Slope of Colorado.* Ouray, CO: Western Reflections, Inc., 1998.

Leonard, Stephen J. *Lynching in Colorado: 1859–1919.* Boulder: University Press of Colorado, 2002.

Marsh, Charles S. *People of the Shining Mountains.* Boulder, CO: Pruett Publishing Co., 1982.

Bibliography

O'Neal, Bill. *Encyclopedia of Western Gunfighters*. Norman: University of Oklahoma Press, 1991.

The Pacific Reporter. Vol. 79. St. Paul, MN: West Publishing Co., 1905.

Pfaelzer, Jean. *Driven Out: The Forgotten War Against Chinese Americans*. New York: Random House, 2007.

Saunders, Gail Zanett, and Maria Jones. *Ouray*. Charleston, SC: Ouray Historical Society and Arcadia Publishing, 2010.

Segrave, Kerry. *Lynchings of Women in the United States: The Recorded Cases, 1851–1946*. Jefferson, NC: McFarland & Company, Inc., 2010.

Smith, Duane A. *The Irrepressible David F. Day*. Lake City, CO: Western Reflections Publishing Co., 2010.

———. *Rocky Mountain Boom Town: A History of Durango, Colorado*. Boulder: University Press of Colorado, 1992.

Stanley, Francis. *The Private War of Ike Stockton*. Denver, CO: World Press, Inc., 1959.

Documents

Callaghan, Thomas J. "Investigation of Colorado Land Fraud Case, 4 April 1939." Report, National Archives, Washington, D.C.

"Maps Recently Published by the U.S. Geological Survey." *National Geographic Magazine* 16 (1905).

Magazines

Thompson, Jonathan. "The Ute Paradox." *High Country News*, 19 July 2010.

Newspapers

Akron (CO) Pioneer Press
Aspen (CO) Times
Aspen (CO) Tribune
Bayfield (CO) Blade

Bibliography

Breckenridge (CO) Bulletin
Colorado Transcript
Denver Republican
Dolores (CO) News
Durango (CO) Democrat
Durango (CO) Herald
Durango (CO) Wage Earner
Fort Collins (CO) Courier
Helena (MT) Independent
Leadville (CO) Daily Herald
Montezuma (CO) Millrun
New York Times
Ouray (CO) Herald
Ouray (CO) Plaindealer
Rocky Mountain Sun (Aspen, CO)
Saguache (CO) Chronicle
Silverite-Plaindealer (Silverton, CO)
Silverton (CO) Standard
Telluride (CO) Daily Journal
Telluride (CO) Journal
Weekly Ignacio (CO) Chieftain
White Pine Cone (Gunnison, CO)

Website

Friedman, S. Morgan. Inflation Calculator. www.westegg.com/inflation (accessed March 14, 2011).

Collection

Hunter, Thomas M., Walter J. Davis, Edward A. Charleton, Joseph A. Langer and Alfred Damon Runyon. "Statement," November 10, 1907. Denver Press Club. Joseph Walker family collection.

About the Author

Carol Turner was born and raised in Colorado and has many Colorado pioneer ancestors. She has a bachelor of arts degree in English from Sonoma State University and a master of fine arts degree in creative writing and literature from Bennington College. She is the author of *Forgotten Heroes and Villains of Sand Creek*, *Notorious Jefferson County* and *Notorious Telluride*. Her short fiction has appeared in numerous literary magazines. She lives in Colorado and writes a history column for the *Broomfield Enterprise* and a Colorado history blog, caturner.wordpress.com. Visit her website at www.carol-turner-books.com.

Photo by Scott E. Olson.

Visit us at
www.historypress.net

www.ingramcontent.com/pod-product-compliance
Lightning Source LLC
Chambersburg PA
CBHW042143160426
43201CB00022B/2391